To Shella
and all dear critters—
With love from Corky and
Pebbles

"Yes, Virginia...
There *IS* a
Pet Heaven"

Understanding
Your Older Dogs and Cats

Corienne 'Corky' Jones

PEBBLES PUBLISHING
Post Office Box 1432
Beaverton, Oregon 97075-1432

Yes, Virginia, There IS a Pet Heaven
by
Corienne 'Corky' Jones

ISBN 0-9631169-0-8
Library of Congress Catalog Card Number: 91-67438

Cover design by Corky Jones and Post Haste Publishing, Inc.
Cover photographs by LAMM Photography
Typeset by Post Haste Publishing, Inc.

Printed in the United States of America

Published by

Pebbles Publishing
Post Office Box 1432
Beaverton, Oregon 97075-1432

10 9 8 7 6 5 4 3 2 1

Notice: All information contained in this book is true, complete, and accurate to the best of our knowledge. All recommendations and suggestions are made without any quarantees on the part of the author or Pebbles Publishing. The author and publisher disclaim all liability incurred in connection with the use of any information or product contained herein.

DEDICATION

*This book is lovingly dedicated to Pebbles, Cricket,
Sara, Sammie, Mandy, Jolie, Leibling, Corkette, Hula, Sherry,
Tucker, and Jackie and to all the dear Seniors
of the many caring dog and cat owners who wrote to me.*

*It is also dedicated to those who are still tenderly caring
for them all—up in Pet Heaven.*

* * *

*An animal companion just has to be one of life's most joyful
and completely rewarding experiences.*

ACKNOWLEDGMENTS

Such a special thank you and deepest appreciation to:

- ~ Laird M. Goodman, D.V.M., Beaverton, OR

- ~ Susan M. Nolte, D.V.M., Beaverton, OR

- ~ Rick Marinelli, N.D. and Elaine Frank, Beaverton, OR

- ~ Donald E. McCoy, D.V.M., Portland, OR

- ~ My inestimable computer guru Pat LeSuer

- ~ My dear friend Charlie Evoy who truly understands the importance of the perfect word!

- ~ Kathi Lamm, photographer par excellence, for the stunning cover photos of my best friend.

- ~ and, of course, my dear Pebbles, always right at my feet during the entire writing of this book.

TABLE OF CONTENTS

FOREWORD

When my beloved Pebbles was almost 15, I started searching for a book that was geared to the special care of older animals. I especially sought one which would give me a better understanding of Pebbles and her aging problems and help me make her later years as pleasant for her as possible. At that time, the only book I found specifically directed to our older pets was *Caring For Older Cats and Dogs* by Robert Anderson, D.V.M. and Barbara J. Wrede. Though an excellent book it didn't give me a lot of the information I was seeking; so Pebbles and I decided we'd write our own!

As we begin this book Pebbles is almost 16. She may or she may not live to see it completed. While I will be utterly devastated when she dies, I will go immediately to our local Humane Society and pray that I again luck out as I did when I adopted Pebbles. (See Chapter 7, "The Adoption")

Pebbles is a fantastic mixed breed of Golden Retriever and Australian Shepherd. She was adopted at age 4 from the Marin Humane Society in Novato, California.

There are wonderful pets of both sexes as well as excellent male and female veterinarians. To eliminate the she/he references, we shall refer to all pets as she (for Pebbles) and vets as he (for Pebbles' vet).

Thanks to the wonderfully nutritious pet foods and the marvelous veterinary care available, our pets are living longer, healthier and happier lives than ever before. I would love to play a big part in assisting all owners of Seniors to make those longer lives just as fulfilling as possible for themselves and their pets.

The aging process and the changes that take place are gradual, starting at about age five to seven years in dogs and cats. Naturally different pets will show the various signs of growing old at different rates. Just wait until you read about Doctor Laird Goodman's cat patient of age 31!

Living with an elderly pet takes a LOT of patience on the part of everyone in the family, not just the pet's primary mistress and care-giver. ALL family members must be educated as to the sometimes difficult times that lay ahead for their Senior, and they must commit themselves to contributing all they possibly can to make the later years of the animal as full of quality life as is possible. If certain family members cannot commit to these conditions it might be best to exclude them from the responsibility for and the care of the animal.

We should treat an aged dog or cat with the same tenderness and compassion as we would any elderly human family member. After all, our beloved Senior IS a treasured family member who has, all its life, given us nothing but unselfish love, devotion, protection and companionship.

It will be most gratifying to me if I can instill in every reader the importance of

EXTRA T.L.C.

COMPASSION AND UNDERSTANDING

PATIENCE + PATIENCE + PATIENCE

WATCHFULNESS

I believe all of us who live with a Senior animal should make up a neat, little card listing the above four points and tack it to the fridge with one of those cutesy magnets. Read it every day and live by it faithfully but, most of all, lovingly.

In no way is this book to be considered a medical textbook. Your own veterinarian is the *only* one you should consult on any health problem that arises.

Pebbles and I are merely relating incidents, experiences and successful remedies. In addition, we hope to be able to alert you to health danger signals and to assist you in understanding them.

While I mention many medicinal products in this book, PLEASE keep in mind that the ONLY one qualified to prescribe for your pet is your own veterinarian. I have discovered several homeopathic remedies that have worked very well for Pebbles and me, and I want to share them with everyone. But, I repeat, only your own vet should make the decision to prescribe any of them for your own dear Senior.

Never give your pet any medicine or preparation suggested to you by a well-meaning friend, simply because it happened to be beneficial to her particular pet.

When I began the happy chore of writing this book, I thought it could take possibly a year or more to complete. (How was I to know — I'd never written a book before!) I had written: "Pebbles is now almost 16. She may or she may not live to see it completed." The book is now almost completed and I am in my final editing mode. Pebbles is doing just beautifully and has been an invaluable co-author! Actually, she believes this book-writing business is pretty neat, since it means that Mom is sure home most of the time.

Jackie

... my very first dog and how I loved her! And did I catch heck when I brought her home unexpectedly!

CHAPTER 1

UNCLE DOCTOR

Your Senior dog or cat's next-best friend is your veterinarian. Not only is he always there to give loving treatment and necessary medication, but he also will always be able to share with you his vast knowledge of everything you should be doing to add many happy and healthy years to your Senior's life. Choose a veterinarian as carefully as you would your own personal medical professional. Look for one with a good, warm "table-side" manner with whom you and your animals have an excellent rapport and are completely comfortable. I believe that finding a vet without these qualifications would be a rarity; I've yet to be associated with a vet that I didn't think was a pretty special person. After all, anyone who wants to spend his life caring for and healing critters can't be all bad!

Your vet will not only be able to advise you on the nutritional needs of your older animal, but also on exactly what to feed and what not to feed. Poor nutrition has a completely negative effect on your Senior's health, resistance to infections, healing of wounds and a variety of injuries, surgeries and illnesses of all kinds. (You can believe your vet is a label reader who knows the very finest of pet foods to recommend to you.)

Your veterinarian is also the *only* one who should counsel you on flea control products. There are hundreds of products on the market many of which are actually harmful to our pets.

With many years of living with your elderly dog or cat, you would know better than anyone what is normal behavior for the pet. When a medical emergency arises, you are the most qualified to give your vet a clear picture of the pet's condition. Be sure to keep a little notebook in which to jot down any abnormalities as they occur. (See Chapter 16.)

When a visit to the vet is in order, be completely honest with him. If he asks if the pet has received the prescribed medication exactly as ordered and perhaps you have missed a dose or two, *confess!* This will assist in his evaluation of the situation. If he has prescribed certain exercises or modes of therapy and you have missed a few sessions, *confess!*

Did you know that you can give CPR to your animals? I didn't until recently, but what a thrilling thing to know! Here again, your vet will be able to instruct you in this life-saving technique.

In the same vein, Emergency Cardiac Massage could very possibly save the life of a beloved Senior if administered by a knowledgeable owner. I pray that it will never happen to you, but it very easily could if your beloved Senior's heart should stop beating. You have a very short time in which to act to save her life (about six minutes). Here again, Uncle Doctor can teach you to give life-saving Emergency Cardiac Massage.

I mention elsewhere the importance of giving your aging female pet a monthly breast exam, just as all women should be giving themselves each month. (It will take a little longer, of course, as there are a few more boobs to explore!) Uncle Doctor will show you exactly how to do the exam with a smooth, short fingernail, so as not to bruise that delicate tissue.

We never want to get into the habit of calling our vet when a Senior sneezes for no apparent reason or doesn't finish all of her breakfast or dinner. When there is a condition or situation of real concern; however, I don't know a vet who would not want you to call him. Better to be safe, than sorry, seems to be the credo of most vets. A veterinarian and dear friend once said to me, "If in doubt, call me."

Many illnesses and conditions of real concern can be detected through the eyes of our animals. The eyes give off danger signals of which we, as Senior owners, must be aware. On your next vet visit, jot each of them down in your trusty little notebook.

The final and probably the most traumatic and saddest encounter you will have with your vet is his assistance in performing euthanasia on your Senior, should it become necessary.

Euthanasia

*"Death is a punishment to some, to some a gift,
and to many a favor."* — *Seneca*

It can never be easy. It is probably one of the most awful times in our entire lives, but it is something that just must be done. Your dear, compassionate veterinarian is there to make it as painless for you as possible. Don't forget...he no doubt loves that Senior almost as much as you do and will no doubt cry right along with you. But he is there, at a time when you need someone by your side with his compassion, his knowledge and his love of your Senior to guide you and to help you through each step of the process to it's final, peaceful end.

I've been so lucky to have met three wonderful veterinarians since moving to Oregon. Dr. Scott Davis of Portland is always such fun to visit just to get a chance to see Iowa. She is his lovely Golden Retriever who carries a piece of her security blanket in her mouth at all times! Thanks to Dr. Susan Nolte of Aloha, Oregon, I learned of Rick Marinelli, N.D. Dr. Marinelli is not a vet, but he certainly is knowledgeable about naturopathic medications for my dog! Thanks to him, and to Gingko Biloba

(See Chapter 26) Pebbles' acute hearing loss was probably 85% restored. Dr. Marinelli also prescribed Zeel for Pebbles' arthritic pain. Our third "Uncle Doctor" is Dr. Laird M. Goodman, a very progressive young man. I would learn of a homeopathic medication for one of Pebbles' ailments, discuss it with Dr. Goodman, who usually knew of the product and what was in it and then we would try it. Laird Goodman is also the vet who has had such good success with acupuncture for animals.

I will always be grateful to Dr. Robert Anderson and Barbara Wrede. It was in their fine book, *Caring For Older Cats and Dogs*, that I first learned of silica for hearing loss. (In addition to the Gingko Biloba, Dr. Marinelli also prescribed Silicea 6X.) Actually, the two products are people medicine, so I've passed the information about them not only to my animal people, but also to many older friends with impaired hearing. I'm delighted to say that I have had some excellent reports on their successful use by both two-legged and four-legged friends.

So, if your Seniors are experiencing any of the health problems that Pebbles has had, talk to your vet about homeopathic medicines. You could gain an abundance of knowledge and, very possibly, alleviate some pain and suffering in your dear Senior's life.

Also, while Pebbles is of the canine persuasion, homeopathic medications are equally as effective for members of the feline persuasion.

Extra T.L.C.
Compassion and Understanding
Patience + Patience + Patience
Watchfulness

CHAPTER 2

YOUR HEALTHY OLDER PET

My last three beloved Seniors all achieved teenager status. Sammie was almost 16 and Mandy was almost 15. Now Pebbles has just had her 16th birthday. I have always attributed their wonderful longevity primarily to Hill's® Science Diet® products, as this is the food they have eaten exclusively. Hill's® Science Diet® produces dog and cat foods for animals of all ages but the Canine Senior kibble is the product that was used in my home as the animals achieved Senior status. It is so complete that the only thing you need add is love.

Shortly after I had decided to write this book, Dr. Susan Nolte gave me a wonderful brochure produced by the Hill's® Company entitled "Your Healthy Older Pet." The brochure offered the following good, sound advice:

> The aging process brings about a gradual reduction in your pet's physical capabilities. While dogs and cats begin to undergo these changes starting at about age five to seven years, different pets will show the various signs of growing old at different rates. The best time to recognize your pet's "senior" status and need

for extra TLC is long before advanced disabilities are apparent.

To increase the length and quality of your pet's life, it is important to begin a process of Risk Factor Management involving both you and your veterinarian. Your veterinarian can help you make a list of your particular dog or cat's "risk factors" so you can begin to manage some or all of them.

The Risks

1. Obesity is one of the single most important risks to the health of the older dog or cat. The tendency for the older pet to gain weight is the result of a slowing of the body's metabolism at the same time that activity level decreases. Obesity is unhealthy in any pet, but is especially harmful to the senior's joints, heart and other organs.

2. Because your pet's metabolism is slowing, you may notice an increasing intolerance to heat and cold. This happens because your pet is now producing less of the hormones which are critical for maintaining the body's normal temperature, regardless of the outside air temperature.

3. Tooth loss and serious gum infections become more common as pets age.

4. Skin problems may occur more frequently because the older pet's skin is less elastic and repairs itself less rapidly.

5. Your pet's senses of sight, smell, taste and hearing will diminish to varying degrees as time passes. Certain diseases of the eyes, like glaucoma and cataracts are more likely in aged pets, and infections or tumors of eyes and

ears may also be serious problems.

6. If your pet has not been neutered earlier in life, problems with various reproductive organs may occur later.

7. Diseases of vital organs like the heart, lungs, kidneys and bladder occur more frequently in the older dog and cat. These organs have been working continuously for many years and will work more slowly or less effectively than before.

Such a good and complete list of the "risk factors" of which we need to be aware should be discussed with our vets.

To further quote from Hill's® brochure:

> The right diet is important at every stage of a pet's life, but never more than during the senior years. Even though your pet may not act much differently, his or her body is going through many changes. These changes influence the type of food an older pet should be fed. Through diet, your veterinarian can help manage the risk of obesity, heart failure, kidney failure, skin and digestive problems and others, by controlling certain nutrients such as sodium, phosphorus, protein and fat. For example, dietary salt intake should be reduced for the older pet while other vital nutrients must be present in a highly available form to meet the senior dog or cat's requirements. The proper diet provides just the right balance of nutrients needed for tissue maintenance and repair, like high quality protein, fatty acids, vitamins and certain minerals. Excesses of nutrients are avoided, reducing the strain on aging vital organs. If your older pet has reduced calorie needs, the proper diet will provide essential nutrients balanced to a higher fiber, lower fat content to reduce the risk of obesity.
>
> Feed only the diet your veterinarian recommends.

Since more "treats" and table foods are high in sodium, you should not permit your "senior" to eat them or any other supplements unless your veterinarian permits them. If you want to reward your pet, feed kibbles of the dry food your veterinarian recommends.

Thank you Hill's® for the permission to present the above vital information to my readers.

EXTRA T.L.C.
COMPASSION AND UNDERSTANDING
PATIENCE + PATIENCE + PATIENCE
WATCHFULNESS

CHAPTER 3

OUR PERSONAL TIMETABLE

When we moved from California to Oregon Pebbles was 13 years old. Up to this point I had observed very few signs of aging, other than some graying around her muzzle. She still ran like a young dog, her coat was beautiful and lustrous, and her appetite was still excellent. It was difficult for me to believe she was 13 years old! (Our new veterinarians couldn't believe she was the age she was.)

After just a few months Pebbles experienced some disturbing symptoms. First, she had a flea problem so pronounced that I had to have the house and grounds professionally sprayed and treated.

Secondly, she developed a very bad skin condition on her tail, which resulted in a great loss of hair and which necessitated constant medication. (See chapter on homeopathic medications, which I learned about some time later.)

During the first few months in our new home she could not stand to have me leave the room. I had a constant "shadow."

By far the most serious development was that Pebbles lost eight pounds! This was *really* disturbing and frightening. Our new vet suggested introducing cooked chicken into her kibble diet. Naturally, she loved it and the weight soon returned to normal.

At that time I knew nothing about stress in our animals lives and had no idea that change in environment could cause such stress. I had always just assumed that Pebbles would be content wherever she was, as long as I was there too.

It turned out that the move from one state to another and from one home to another was a very stressful event for my beloved dog. I have since read much about the importance and complications of stress in older animals when their environment is changed.

At about 14-1/2 years, Pebbles was getting up in the mornings and lying down a bit slower. Also, those usual long stretches in the morning were not as evident.

At age 15, she seemed to be sleeping more and developing some strange little habits. I don't believe that our animals become senile, as we know senility in humans, as they age. They are simply slowing down physically and, probably, mentally. There must be a lot of confusion in their minds as these changes take place.

Although, a question such as "Want to go in the car with me?" will very possibly get the same degree of excitement and loving anticipation in a 15-year-old as it will in a 1-year old!

On Pebbles' 15th birthday, her birthday gift from me was a trip to beautiful Cannon Beach, not too far from Beaverton. She had not run free on a beach in over a year. Any observer of this big, golden beauty would never have believed she was 15 years old! She acted more like a 2-year-old and had one of the best days of her life.

I decided then to promise Pebbles a trip to the beach at least once a month ... that is, until I discussed it with our good Dr. Laird Goodman. While Pebbles loved her romp on the beach, it really was not doing her arthritis much good, and more pain could probably result. (She conked out the entire trip back home, about one and one-half hours, and she did seem a bit stiff the next day.)

So, our older pets need more not less exercise as they age, but definitely in moderation. A hard run on the beach, however enjoyable, may not be beneficial.

At around age 15-1/2, Pebbles experienced pronounced hearing loss. (See Chapter 15 and 26 on homeopathic remedies for *good* news on this subject.)

After a two month use of two *natural* medications, Pebbles' hearing was so markedly improved it was amazing. (Thank you, Dr. Rick Marinelli. We love you!)

- Pebbles would awaken and lift her head when I would sneeze.

- She would awaken and lift her head in the morning when I would turn off the electric blanket.

- In the past where she could not hear the jingle of her collar when I put it on in the mornings, she could later hear it from across the large living room.

When Pebbles was age 15-1/2, our vet prescribed DES for considerable urine incontinence. It was used for about 3 weeks, until I read in Dr. Anderson's book that DES can cause side effects. I stopped the medication and, happily, the incontinence did not return. I would have next tried a homeopathic preparation, but there seemed to be no need.

When Pebbles was about 15-1/2, there were definite bowel problems. (Please see Chapter 4, Bowels And Other Fascinating Topics)

Extra T.L.C.
Compassion and Understanding
Patience + Patience + Patience
Watchfulness

BOWELS AND OTHER FASCINATING TOPICS

Talk to your animals — they love it!

I have always talked to my animals, yes, frequently in baby-talk too! Why not? Four-legged critters are, after all, important members of your family.

Just recently, I read an article about that fabulous animal lover and trainer, Gunther Gebel-Williams. One of his comments was memorable: "People disappoint you, but animals never do."

THINK ABOUT THAT!

As I was saying, your pets love to be talked to at any age, but as they grow older, they need constant reassurance that you love them dearly. While their bodies are going through some strange changes that they can't possibly comprehend, the voice of the person nearest and dearest to them has much therapeutic benefit.

Many's the time I've gotten down on the floor next to Pebbles' bed when she has seemed to be upset or stressed. I don't necessarily need to touch her, and I'm perhaps a foot or two away from her. I just talk to her; I tell her what a good girl she is, how much I love her, and that I hope tomorrow will be a better day, with no aches and pains. There have been times when she has been panting at the onset of our "discussion," and, after a few minutes of my talking quietly and calmly to her, the panting has subsided.

In these little intimate moments, one reason why I don't feel it is necessary to have physical contact with my animal is that there are times when they *don't want or need to be touched.* They need their "space" too. We can overdo the constant desire to pet and stroke them. Haven't you had times when you feel pretty rotten and you just don't want *anyone* even to touch you, as good as their intentions may be? But, those loving words from the dearest person in that animal's life are usually always welcome.

Remember the dear English lady on television (gosh, how I miss her!), who stressed how terribly important the spoken word was to your dog, and the truly marvelous results that she achieved from just that formula.

Yes, I have *always* spoiled my animals — but *why not!* When Pebbles and I moved from California to Oregon, my girl saw snow for the first time (to my knowledge) in her life. The nights were extremely cold, and leaving the nice, warm fire in the family room to go back to our bedroom at bed-time was not always terribly pleasant. I used to put a big, fluffy beach towel in the clothes dryer for several minutes until it was nice and warm, and then lay it on her bed. That had to feel pretty good! This could also be a very welcome touch whenever an animal has come in out of the cold, or when it's recovering from an illness or a surgery.

Panting

It was not until Pebbles became a Senior that I learned that panting can not only mean too-warm weather (naturally) but also it can sometimes denote that pain is present. When Pebbles panted and I knew it wasn't caused by weather conditions, I wanted to learn why. Dr. Goodman furnished me with the following explanations:

> Because dogs don't have sweat glands, (except on their feet), panting is the mechanism whereby they can give off excess heat. Besides indicating that they are warm, dogs will also pant when they are nervous or stressed.
>
> In addition, older dogs may pant due to normal aging changes occurring in the lungs. As the dog matures, fibrous or scar-type tissue is laid down in the air waves (bronchi and bronchioles). This makes the lungs less resilient and dogs often need to pant to move appropriate amounts of air through the lungs.

Bowel Incontinence

At about age 15-1/2, Pebbles demonstrated some unusual bowel malfunctions. At first, I thought it was because of stress caused when I left her at home alone. Sometimes there would be "droppings" either on the living room carpet or in the hall between the living room and the rest of the house. By process of elimination (No pun intended!), I later determined that this loss of bowel control was directly related to Pebbles' being left home alone. She could see, through the front window, when my car approached. From the living room she would then start down the long hall to the door that led to the garage entrance. All along this trip to "greet Mom" was a series of poops. It was evident that, in her excitement, she had lost control of her bowels. There was *never* any scolding or displeasure on my part as I simply picked up the "calling cards" with the convenient napkins and flushed them down the toilet. Then, I told my girl how glad

I was to see her and that she was a good girl. At times like this, *please* don't scold. Your animal knows that she has done something unacceptable, but she couldn't prevent it. Again, I am just grateful that Pebbles' bowels still function without the need for constipation medication.

Bowels

An interesting variation on Pebbles' droppings incident led me to believe that just possibly she was unhappy with me and was going to retaliate in her own special way. One day when I had an early appointment, I dressed very quietly and was practically ready to leave when she finally awakened, about 9:00 am. She knew immediately by the way I was dressed that I was going out, and the look on her face let me know in no uncertain terms that she was not in favor. I tried to put her out again (she had been out at 7:00 when I first got up), but she refused. I fixed her breakfast and went back to the bedroom for shoes. When I returned a few minutes later there were several poops on the family room floor. Again, without scolding her, I simply picked them up and flushed them away. Now more than ever, I believe Pebbles' depositing of the "calling cards" is associated with the stress of being left alone.

On occasion there will be one little poop on Pebbles' bed in the morning. Also, sometimes when she's crossing the deck on her way to the back yard, she can't quite make it to the yard and will drop poops on the deck. NO PROBLEM! There's always a supply of paper napkins right by the back door.

Security

I was recently told by a local police officer, as he pointed to Pebbles, "That family member cuts your chances of being burglarized by about 75%!"

I have always believed this to be true. Many years ago in California, I had two miniature poodles, Sammie and Mandy. Though small, they were very vocal whenever anyone approached the house, and that was just fine with me. Over a period of time the homes on either side of me were burglarized, but we never once had such an incident. Having lived alone for many years, I would never dream of living without a dog, not only for the sheer joy of their companionship and love, but also for the feeling of protection that one is given.

Following

Since her 16th birthday, Pebbles' need for my constant companionship seems to be more pronounced. When I leave the family room to walk down the hall to another room or when I leave the office to walk a few feet across the hall to the bathroom, she simply must follow, even though I give her the command to "stay." Once in a great while she will remain on her bed and await my return, which is usually within three or four minutes. It saddens me to think she experiences such feelings of insecurity, but, on the other hand, I welcome that extra bit of exercise she gets so often.

During the day when Pebbles spends most of her time on her living room bed (if I'm not working in the studio) and I am in the family room, about every 20 minutes she will make a little round trip in from the living room and through the kitchen to see that I am still there. She then returns to her bed in the living room.

Pet Stain Removal

There are just one or two good products on the market for the removal of pet accidents on carpets or rugs. A word of caution: check the ingredients carefully and never buy one that lists ammonia, as it will not work for your dogs or your cats.

Pet Doors

I have very mixed emotions regarding the use of pet doors. They are fine if you are home and just need to eliminate constant letting in and out, or if you have a very secure yard. I would not rely on a pet door if I were still a working person, unless I had a yard secure enough to prevent anyone from entering, or tossing anything into the yard. I may be needlessly cautious, but there are just too many weird people running around loose these days.

Aspirin

Many veterinarians will prescribe good old aspirin for pain relief for dogs. This is fine. Never take it upon yourself to give it or any other human medication to an animal. And, NO aspirin for cats, as it can be very toxic to them.

Compassion

Our animals, especially our dogs and cats, can be so compassionate and understanding of our most inner feelings that it is uncanny.

A few years ago, I was quite ill with a severe depression. There were several instances where I would be sitting on the couch, doing nothing, but experiencing a feeling of total despair. Pebbles, lying on her bed across the room, would stare at me for a moment or two, then walk over, put one paw on my knee and just look at me. In all this world there was never more love and compassion than that in those beautiful big eyes. Pebbles helped me through countless bad, bad times which I honestly don't believe I would have survived otherwise without this amazing animal. (There seemed to be no family members willing to give me a much-needed paw!)

The incident when I was burying Mandy in the back yard showed again the uncanny depth of Pebbles' feelings. She sensed my sadness and came to me with her magic paw to give me comfort. Some day, I hope I will meet and spend some time with someone who really understands and can explain to me these amazing animal brains!

Incontinence Products

Incontinence in our pets can be an extremely difficult situation for all concerned; the animal is embarrassed and distressed; and it can be frustrating at times for the owner, trying to mop up beds, floors, carpets and car seats. Should the condition arise, first have your vet check to see what is causing the incontinence. At times it can be a bladder or kidney infection that can be easily treated. If the condition is purely age-related, you must just live with it. There are, however, a couple of products on the market to make the situation a bit easier to cope with. I have noted them in two very good pet supply catalogs from ANIMAIL and R. C. STEELE. One is a type of diaper for pets which works on the same principle as the ones we used to put on our kids' bottoms. The other is an abbreviated pants design into which you insert a small sanitary napkin, replacing it as needed. Either concept could certainly make life more pleasant with a serious incontinence problem.

Sometimes older spayed females and, less commonly, older neutered males experience hormonal incontinence. Happily, your vet can diagnose and treat this condition.

Safety Sticker

Another great product available is the Safety Sticker. This is a sticker you place on a window or door near the front and back entrances to your home. It announces that there is a pet (or pets) in the home, alerting firemen, for instance, in case of fire or any other emergency within the home. I have used these little stickers for years. Our Marin Humane Society used to make them available at nominal cost. When I could no longer obtain them, I had some inexpensively printed up to tape in the appropriate spots, and I also passed them on to friends who owned pets.

Maggie From San Anselmo

I was very pleased to hear about Maggie, a 12-year-old Angora/Siamese from my old home-town of San Anselmo, California. Donna Lazarus wrote such a charming letter giving me a detailed account of Maggie's routine. I loved her description of a typical after-dinner happening: "After dinner is face grooming, low-impact aerobics, stretching, and some feline gymnastics, scoring a perfect 10 each time." Can't you just picture it? Donna's closing paragraph pretty much sums up the way we all feel about our beloved pets: "In summary, she doesn't work, pay bills, clean house, do errands or argue; instead she makes our house a home, warns us of visitors with her keen hearing, lowers our blood-pressure with her constant loving, and all in all, is great company."

Blood Pressure

Speaking of blood-pressure, it has been proven that visits to nursing homes by both dogs and cats HAVE been instrumental in lowering the blood pressure of the residents. Not only that but these elderly people also benefit physically in many other ways. I would love to see the day come when nursing homes will have a pet or two as welcome residents.

One aspect of Pebbles' behavior for which I have absolutely no explanation was her strange routine during the last "out" of the evening, usually around 11:00 pm. (This began about two weeks after her 16th birthday.) I would take her out the back door to her yard area and give the usual command "go potty." In the past, the command always got almost immediate results. However, for some reason, she began the unusual behavior of walking a few feet, then coming back to the deck area. I would give the command again, she would walk a few feet, and then again try to return to the back door. Some nights this would go on for 10 to 15 minutes, concerned as I was that she "go," before we went to bed for the night. I don't know if the outdoor lights were bothering her (I always tried to stay in a position where she could see me), or if she was having a real problem seeing well. On more than one occasion, I would finally give up trying to force her to urinate, as I didn't want to stress her too badly. We would go to bed and there was never an accident during the night; but I could never understand how she could go for that many hours without the usual late-night trip out.

Extra T.L.C.
Compassion and Understanding
Patience + Patience + Patience
Watchfulness

CHAPTER 5

TURN NEGATIVES INTO POSITIVES

When little occurrences tend to be annoying or to try your patience, always do your best to turn a negative into a positive.

Bowel Incontinence

When your dear, old friend loses bowel control once in a while on the carpet, be grateful that she is still "moving" naturally and without the aid of laxative medication. It just takes a minute to pick up these little calling cards. Above all, no scolding or reprimanding! Most dogs (and probably cats, too) are truly embarrassed at making a mistake in an unacceptable area.

MORAL: Never buy or wear an article of clothing without pockets; for when you live with a dear Senior pet, they will always need to be filled with paper napkins.

"Out" Constantly

When your Senior asks to "go out" four times in half an hour, be grateful that she has not forgotten all your good earlier training and is attempting to do the right thing. Even if there is no elimination, be grateful for that extra exercise the pet is getting!

> *MORAL:* If you're a Senior too, the extra steps generally can't hurt you either!

Following

When your elderly pet insists on following you when you go from room to room, or each time you leave the room for the bathroom, be grateful again for all that exercise she is getting. (Especially in rainy weather.)

> *MORAL:* Who else in your life has ever been concerned about whether or not you made it to the john?

Urine Incontinence

There aren't too many positives if your dear Senior suffers from urine incontinence, and it's sure not too much fun cleaning up the accidents. However, it IS infinitely better than a kidney or bladder ailment resulting in the inability to urinate.

EXTRA T.L.C.
COMPASSION AND UNDERSTANDING
PATIENCE + PATIENCE + PATIENCE
WATCHFULNESS

CHAPTER 6

ACHES AND PAINS
AND A FEW RELIEFS

Probably the saddest old-age ailment to see develop in your Senior is arthritis, and it seems to be so common in both cats and dogs. (Having had arthritic problems myself over the past few years, I know the pain involved.)

Shortly after her 15th birthday, Pebbles was getting up and lying down much more slowly. There was obvious pain in both functions. I remembered a statement made by Dr. Robert Anderson in *Caring For Older Cats and Dogs*: "Consider yourself fortunate if you live within driving distance of a competent veterinary acupuncturist."

I was indeed fortunate, since I had only recently heard of Dr. Laird M. Goodman, who was having excellent results using acupuncture. I made an appointment for Pebbles to have the preliminary X-rays, and we started a series of three acupuncture treatments. There was undoubtedly some relief from pain, but not the dramatic results that we had seen in many of Dr. Goodman's other Senior patients. As he explained to me, acupuncture does not work for all animals, and you will generally know after about three treatments if it will be successful for your animal. (Pebbles' arthritis was in the spine.) [Note: In a recent talk with Doctor Goodman, he told me that frequently cats respond quicker to acupuncture than do dogs.]

One home remedy that I tried (and still use) seemed to give some pain relief: I simply laid a heating pad (on low setting) over her entire back for ten minutes two or three times a day. I would sit on the floor with her, telling her what a good patient she was, and she took each treatment very calmly. (Or, if my arthritic knee was acting up, I would sit on a chair just above where she was lying.)

And, don't forget, obesity will hasten and aggravate an arthritic condition in any of us!

If your Senior suffers from arthritis, ask your vet about slowly and gently flexing each leg for several minutes each day.

Comfort Mattress

You have no doubt seen the blue, egg-crate, foam rubber mattresses that are used on patients' beds in hospitals. They are also available for our pets in various animal catalogs, but are quite expensive. If you are lucky enough to know someone connected with a hospital, perhaps you can obtain one of these marvelous items. A single bed mattress can be cut in half for good-sized beds. (If your animal is small, several can be cut from one mattress.) I also learned from my computer guru that they are available in such stores as K-Mart and Target at around $10.00. (I would imagine that many of the larger drug chains also carry such items.) Also, watch for sales, as I recently saw a twin-size mattress advertised for $6.99. Slip-covers can be fashioned from an old sheet or any sturdy, cotton, easily washable fabric.

Pebbles loved her new beds immediately (one permanently in the living room and one in our bedroom which gets moved to the studio when I will be in there for a length of time). Not only does this type of bed help relieve aching joints, the pain of hip dysplasia and arthritis, but also the animals' weight is more evenly distributed and circulation is improved. This type of bed is also a real comfort to a dog or cat recovering from an injury or surgery.

Cortisone

One morning, Pebbles was suddenly limping severely with her right front paw. I examined the foot and leg, but could find nothing, so off we went to Dr. Goodman. After his examination to rule out any cause other than arthritis, he suggested a Cortisone injection. It was beneficial for over a week. I still see her limp occasionally for just about 30 to 40 seconds after she has gotten up from lying down. (Cortisone is effective in acute flare-ups of arthritic pain; however, Dr. Goodman generally does not recommend its long-term use in controlling arthritic pain. The drug can cause negative effects on other organs and the arthritic pain can be worsened.)

DMSO

We also tried DMSO for close to a month for the spinal arthritis. I don't know how beneficial this was. Next we used Dismutase (Superoxide), which was more to my liking since it is a natural product, as opposed to a drug. This did not seem to give the pain relief to Pebbles that I was so desperately trying to find.

Zeel

Once when I was in Dr. Marinelli's office picking up Pebbles' hearing medications, Elaine told me about Zeel, a most effective homeopathic medication for arthritis in humans. I wondered about trying it for a four-legged patient. After discussing it with Dr. Goodman and showing him literature on

Zeel, we decided to try it next for Pebbles' arthritis. (Dr. Marinelli prescribed one tablet, three times a day, plus one teaspoon of cod liver oil daily.) *In one week,* I could see marked improvement in Pebbles: she was obviously in less pain, getting up and lying down more easily; and, instead of sleeping in until 10:00 am, she was getting up between 8:00 and 8:45 am. In addition, there was much more enthusiasm and activity first thing in the morning, especially at breakfast time. I don't know if there is any connection between the new arthritis medication and her bowel functions, but, for about a week, there was no bowel incontinence in the house! (It is now happening again, occasionally, seems to be directly related to my leaving the house without her.)

Here again, a natural homeopathic medicine. Among the ingredients are homeopathic botanical substances, (Arnica montana, and Rhus toxicodendron) and homeopathic mineral substances such as sulfur. If arthritis is a problem in your pet's life (or your own), you might want to discuss Zeel with your vet and a naturopathic physician. I think it's a winner!

If you have an arthritic Senior dog or cat, always remember:

MORE T.L.C. THAN EVER BEFORE …

… but gentle hugs and stroking. Remember there may be lots of pain. And don't lift the animal's head up abruptly, as this can be painful to an arthritic back. Caution any visitors, perhaps meeting your Senior for the first time, to administer very gentle petting and stroking.

Foot Pads

At about age 15-1/2, Pebbles seemed to be walking rather gingerly over an area in our back yard that had a path made up of large river rocks. (She had to cross this path to reach her toilet area.)

I decided that those little foot pads, after years of fetching, searching, running, hiding, chasing and beach-combing just had to be getting sore. With a piece of green indoor-outdoor carpeting I covered the area where she crossed over the rocks eliminating that little inconvenience. (The carpeting is not very expensive, can easily be hosed off when soiled and, of course, will not be hurt by the weather.)

Slippery Flooring

As our Senior dogs age, their hind legs lose so much of their strength and they can lose control of the hind quarters, so eliminating very smooth and slick surfaces is important. A bad fall could easily result in a broken or painfully sprained leg or foot. Since much of our home was finished in hardwood floors, Pebbles often slipped and floundered, especially while racing to the front door at the sound of the doorbell or jumping around in the kitchen as I carried her meals to the utility room. I purchased two long lengths of heavy plastic floor runners and placed them over the areas that could have become real hazard areas. It solved the problem nicely.

Failing Eyesight

For several years Pebbles' eyes have been quite cloudy and our Uncle Doctor recently found evidence of cataracts. I know that cataract surgery in pets is quite common and usually successful, but at this stage of Pebbles' life, I don't believe that I would subject her to surgery. There are times I am aware of her failing eyesight; however, she can *still* locate a single dropped kibble on the floor if I simply point to it!

If you leave one room to go into another and your shadow follows, as Pebbles does constantly, be sure that there is sufficient light in the room so that your Senior can see you. I have seen panic in my dog's eyes if I have gone into the bathroom, for example, and not turned on the light so that she can locate me.

If your Senior's eyesight is really bad, she can still function very well indeed. Just try not to rearrange furniture or to make any major changes in your home.

When a move to a new home or apartment is necessary, it is a simple task to educate the animal (cat or dog) by patiently and repeatedly showing her just where everything is located, including all door openings.

Increased Water Consumption

In a recent visit with Uncle Dr. Goodman, (he has been SO helpful to me in the compiling of this book), he mentioned the importance of noting increased water consumption by your older dog or cat. This can be a danger signal of which you must be aware. Jot down the pertinent facts in your trusty little notebook and advise your vet right away of a marked increase in water consumption.

Chocolate

During this same visit, while we were discussing nutrition, I also learned that chocolate is toxic to our animals! I have always known that anything containing sugar was no-no-no for our animals, but I didn't realize how dangerous chocolate could be! (Also toxic are several plants, among them being mistletoe and poinsettia.)

EXTRA T.L.C.

COMPASSION AND UNDERSTANDING

PATIENCE + PATIENCE + PATIENCE

WATCHFULNESS

Diabetes In Dogs & Cats

Another of the devastating illnesses that can attack both our dogs and cats is diabetes. While it can occur as early as age six months, it is generally seen in animals between seven and ten years, and the obese animals are more likely to succumb to the disease than are those of proper body weight.

Strokes

Strokes, though not too common, do occur in older animals. As a rule, they are not life-threatening, so never consider having your animal put to sleep if one should occur. They frequently are of short duration and the recovery period can be very fast.

Have your vet talk to you about the signs of a stroke on your next visit.

Recently Pebbles acted rather strangely, which prompted me to wonder if she had suffered a very mild stroke. One evening she arose from her bed very shakily, her hind legs were quite unsteady, and as she walked, she carried her tail well off to one side. Everything was back to normal within several minutes; however, I did mention the occurrence to Uncle Doctor on our next visit.

CHAPTER 7

ADOPTIONS — AND ESPECIALLY PEBBLES' ADOPTION

On April 13, 1979, my beloved poodle Sammie died at age almost 16.

On July 31, 1979, my beloved poodle Mandy died at age almost 15.

On Monday, August lst, I called the Marin Humane Society to see what adult female dogs were available for adoption. On Friday afternoon I went out to find my new friend.

The following is a true accounting of the next two and one-half days, as told by my lovely new Golden Retriever/Australian Shepherd, Pebbles, age 4.

The Adoption

There were about twelve of us waiting to be adopted at the Humane Society that Friday afternoon. She looked at all of us, but she stopped at our kennel the longest (the one I shared with Misty, the young Black Labrador).

She took me out first and I knew right away she would be a neat lady to live with! I tried so hard to please her; I didn't bark, I didn't jump on her, and I swished my magnificent tail constantly! I knew she liked me because she asked all kinds of questions of Tom, our nice kennel man: how much to feed me, how much exercise I would need, did he think I could be an "inside" dog while she was at her office. (I hadn't ever been an "inside" dog, but I sure could become one for her!) She was a little bit concerned that I was four years old, I think, because she said something to Tom about "that Misty" being only one year old. (She's really just a kid, and not the calm, refined lady that I am.)

Then she took me back to the kennel and took "that Misty" out and they were gone for such a long time! My heart pounded — I prayed so hard that she would choose me. We were so right for each other! I would be so loving, I would protect her, I would try so hard to be everything she wanted me to be! I also heard her tell Tom she was going to take a week of her vacation next week to spend with her new friend. Gosh, to think we would have nine whole days together!

Then "that Misty" came back to the kennel, but she didn't and she was away for the longest time and then, finally, she walked up to Misty and me again. I gave her a few of those looks that only a Golden Retriever can give! (I'm only Golden on Mother's side of the family, and I sure have her eyes!) It just took a couple of my most expressive eyebrow messages and I knew she was mine! She left then and went back out to the Adoption Desk. My heart was pounding again when she left, but I knew she'd be back!

She had to sign some papers and then Tom came and got me and put on the collar and leash she had brought, and off we went to her car. I was nervous about the car at first, but I got in and I was a perfect lady in the back seat.

On the way home we had to stop at her vet's office, where she picked up a little wooden box. Also, she wanted him to meet me and he thought I was just beautiful and said I was very healthy. (Now there was a vet with good taste!)

Finally, we got to our house and there was a bed for me in the kitchen, one in the living room and one in our bedroom! There were some nice chewing toys and a couple of lovely, big bones, (Although I didn't know very much about toys, I would probably learn what they were for.) There was a nice spot in the kitchen where she gave me a bowl of water and where she'll probably put my meals. (Bet she's a good cook, too.)

My first evening in my lovely new home was sheer heaven! We had a nice walk, she petted me a lot, she told me how beautiful I was, and what a dinner I had! (Some difference between having your very own home and mistress and the past ten days with "that Misty.")

When it was time for us to go to bed, she showed me where my bed was, over on the side of the room. For my tastes, it was a bit too far from her — I wanted to be right next to her bed! So, she moved mine. (I can see she'll be quite easy to train!)

Several times during the night I felt her hand reach down for me and I gave a few thumps with my big tail. I raised my head and gave her hand a nice lick, but I didn't get up or try to get on the bed, as I had tried that earlier and was told that ON the bed was NO.

The next day was full of all sorts of good things! I explored every inch of my nice, big yard, I had another good walk, she brushed me (I wasn't used to that and it pulled sometimes, but I never moved an inch), and we just enjoyed each other.

That second evening something sort of strange happened. She went out to our back yard and dug a hole and was putting this little wooden box into it. She seemed to be crying at the same time and I couldn't really understand, since she had seemed so happy with me all day. I went to her and put my paw on her knee and gave her a big, slurpy kiss. (We Goldens always seem to know the proper thing to do, you know.) That seemed to make everything all right again and then we went back into our house and I had my second good dinner and another loving evening.

It's been two and a half days now. I no longer get up to follow her every time she leaves the room, I know she'll be back in a minute. The only time I've cried was once when we were in the back yard and she went into the house and I hadn't yet learned how to open the screen door. I haven't barked once, but I hope she doesn't think I can't! Just let someone try to come into our house or try to harm her! You want barking? I'll give you barking.

This morning, Sunday, we had another long walk. Then she had some errands, so I rode in our car again and now I rather like it. Once, she had to leave me in the car; but she found a shady spot to park and I had lots of windows open, so I was most comfortable. But was I happy when we started home and came to our driveway and to our front door! It's always nice to travel, but there's just no place like your own home.

Footnote: Late Sunday evening, while we were relaxing in our living room, I looked down on this truly beautiful, sleeping dog and simply admired her. I said (quietly, I thought), "Thank God I found you and thank God I was able to keep you from the fate of euthanasia." She didn't open her eyes or move at all — she just thumped that big, golden tail twice.

Adoptions — And Especially Pebbles'

I have heard from so many people whose adopted dogs and cats seem to be extra-special pets. They seem to know that, because of you, their lives have been saved and are now going to be pretty wonderful. They seem to want to express, in so many different ways, that they are grateful. Having known Pebbles and several other adopted pets all these years, I know this to be true.

Each animal that I have lived with over the past 40 years has been loving, devoted, protective and, in every way, my best friend. But there has been a distinct difference in animals that I have adopted as well as my other best friend who came to me courtesy of Guide Dogs For the Blind, Inc. in San Rafel, California. (See Chapter 14 on Guide Dogs)

From day one Pebbles showed me love and devotion, but her immediate and distinctive display of protectiveness was really quite amazing.

We had been in our home together for approximately two hours when my dear, little friend Carol Foutz (one of California's greatest miniaturists) came to call and to meet Pebbles. It was August, so the front door was open leaving just the screened door closed. I was on the telephone when Carol arrived, so I motioned for her to come on in. Pebbles was lying on the floor by the couch on which I was seated.

Carol came in the door and started to walk towards me, arms out-stretched, saying "Oh, she's beautiful!" Pebbles immediately jumped up on the couch, separating Carol from me, and snarled at poor little Carol, all five feet of her! Carol was devastated and was so sure Pebbles would never accept or love her; but Pebbles, right from the beginning of our life together, was simply protecting me from a stranger whom she thought might have been a threat to me. Those two turned out to be dear friends for many years, because no animal alive could not love Carol Foutz and vice versa.

The point here is the immediate feeling of protectiveness this animal felt for me, after having been with me for a little over two hours. Pebbles' protectiveness of me has been constant throughout all the years we have been together. Whenever anyone came to the front door, unless I said "It's o.k., it's a friend," that person would not get through the door. When there was a serviceman in the house, Pebbles always positioned herself between that person and me. I hate to think of what might have happened to anyone who had tried to harm me physically!

Looking back over the many years spent with Pebbles, the only other time I ever saw her snarl at anyone was one time when someone made a menacing approach to our car in which she was seated alone. Generally, there never was a more laid-back and mellow lady.

All I knew about Pebbles when I adopted her was that she had been a farm dog. The previous owners had too many dogs, and Pebbles didn't get along too well with the livestock. She has always been on the timid side, and I think possibly she might have been kicked by a horse or a cow at some time. Although I could never understand how anyone could have given up an animal such as this, I was grateful to the former owners for taking her to the Humane Society so that another loving home could be found for her. Boy, did I luck out that day!

It would be the answer to a profound prayer if Pebbles' former family would read this book and know what a beautiful life she has had and the utter joy she has brought to my life all these years!

Pebbles was never interested in all the things we buy for our pets' pleasure like chew toys or balls with bells. (Being a former farm dog, I doubt that she was ever given toys of any kind.) So her only Christmas present each year was a huge box of dog biscuits, which she always opened herself. She would get the ribbon and wrapping paper off and then start in on the cardboard top. At this point I would remove the box with the biscuits to be doled out at appropriate times.

However, at about age 15-1/2, after having read in another animal book about how beneficial the rawhide bones were for a dog's teeth, I decided to try again. I purchased a large one for Pebbles. She must have decided that I wasn't being as proficient as I had hoped to be in the teeth-cleaning department, since she accepted it and started chewing on it. Later, from time to time she would pick it up of her own accord and chew on it. It was as if she were doing it just to please me. (Actually, the rawhide bones are good for chewing exercise and for promoting jaw strength, but they are not really helpful for cleaning the teeth.)

One more example of ESP between Pebbles and me occurred in the second week that we had been together. I had taken a vacation week the first week so that we could have a good long time to get acquainted and settled in, but then it was time for me to return, reluctantly, to my job. The back yard was fenced in, I had had a "dog door" installed in back, and the back gate was securely locked. I drove out the driveway and down the street about one block. Something told me to stop and wait, which, thank God, I did. In approximately four minutes, who should come racing down the driveway, and down the street towards my car but Pebbles!

Back home we went and immobilized the dog door so that she could not do it again. She would have to stay in the house until my return. That evening I was fortunate enough to get help in building up the back gate about four more feet, so that she could never jump over it again. We never had a problem such as this again, and my point is that I knew what this dog was going to do five minutes after I had left her.

Another example of how deeply our animals feel and how completely they understand when we are displeased with them is the "Apple Tree Incident." Pebbles had been with me about a year when she did something very naughty (for the life of me, I can't remember what it was, but I was very unhappy with her). I told her what a bad girl she was and I believe it was really the only time I was actually mad at her in all the years we were together! Crushed, she turned and walked about 25 feet up into the back yard and laid down under the apple tree. I was doing some work which took me in and out of the house several times. Pebbles would raise her head whenever I came outside and put it down again when I left, but otherwise never moved. She stayed under the apple tree for two hours! Finally, I could stand her obvious grief no longer and called her to me, telling her that I still loved her, and that all was forgiven.

> *MORAL:* An animal (especially a dog) never has to be physically punished; just some very harsh words showing displeasure are all that are usually needed.

Here is more on the subject of Pebbles' adoption from the Marin Humane Society. One of the reasons that Pebbles had been there for a long ten days (and not the usual four or five) was that she was so wonderful with all the volunteers, young and old. They would use her as a "patient" when they gave demonstrations on first aid, etc., and they all told me that they could do absolutely anything with her because of her beautiful temperament.

CHAPTER 8

HER ROYAL HIGHNESS — THE CONTESSA

I've known a lot of happy families in my lifetime, but I've never known a happier one than the one I met recently in a warm, loving little home in Portland. Perhaps the composition of this particular family was a bit unusual, but the devotion and total love of one for the other in this home was a joy to see.

This delightful family consists of Mom, Pat McClure, a trim, tan, vibrant, little widow; Contessa, a gorgeous Siamese of 31 years; and Cocko, Chrissie, Gabby, Rusty and Nipper.

Some of these dear critters had been rescued from life-threatening situations by Pat to become beloved members of her family. Pat is the type of lady who will take into her home and her heart just about any animal in need of a safe, secure and loving home.

Gabby, another beautiful Siamese, aged 8, was rescued from a pretty stress-filled existence and in deplorable condition. Today she sure lives the good life, and deservedly so! One of the joys of her life is "Toy-Toy": it's a long stick with a string on the end to which is attached a colorful bouncing toy and it's kept in a closet just off the living room. No matter where Gabby might be, the minute Pat says "Toy-Toy," quick as a Siamese flash,

Gabby is at the closet door. The day I visited, Gabby was asleep on the back of a couch. Pat said the magic words and Gabby was awake in an instant and bounding to the closet door.

Of all the animals, Gabby is the only one with a real health problem: she has Leukemia, which, thankfully, is in remission.

Cocko, age 5, is a lovely black long-haired cat who lived under Pat's house for about six months before deciding Pat would be a pretty neat gal to live with. I feel Cocko was destined to find Pat and her family. After hearing a few stories Pat had to tell about her beloved Satan, a wonderful cat, who departed this life at age 17, I can't help but believe that Cocko is the reincarnation of Satan. There are just too many coincidences for it not to be true!

Chrissie, the baby of the family at two years old, is a delightful, black, long-haired kitty. She's a sweetheart and so friendly.

And then there is Nipper, age 3. Nipper was rescued, as a baby, from under a bush in the front yard during a severe rain storm. She was more dead than alive when Pat just happened to see her. She took the frightened little critter in the house, dried her, comforted her, and then called the veterinarian, our beloved Dr. Laird Goodman, to see how she should proceed with the animal's care. For, you see, Nipper was a Ferret!

Nipper is litter-box trained, romps and plays with all the cats, is so loving and gentle and returns to her living room cage on command. She is quite lovely, very similar to a Siamese in coloring. It was a thrill to meet her, as I had never ever seen a Ferret before. You haven't lived until you've had a gentle little kiss in the ear by a Ferret!

The last member of this wonderful family is Rusty, age 3. Rusty is a delightfully bouncy and loving combination of Springer Spaniel and Cocker Spaniel, and he is a great, vocal watchdog.

As for Contessa, age 31, what a real treat it was to meet this loving, healthy and amazing kitty! When I received a letter from

Peggy Coleman and Grammie, her 25-year-old cat, I thought that was pretty spectacular. Then, to learn about Contessa! I just had to meet her, and Pat McClure graciously allowed me to pay a visit to this great family.

Contessa

... still a most important member of Pat McClure's great family at age 31.

Outside of a strange infection that appears about every ten years, Contessa is in wonderful health. (Pat, you sure must be doing everything right!) She does have cataracts, which don't slow her down much; her hearing is still pretty good and Pat tells me her teeth are very good. It was a real treat for me to be able to meet this delightful kitty and her Mom.

When a human family member reaches age 90, he sometimes receives a nice card from the President. When our four-legged family members also reach a pretty spectacular age, wouldn't it be nice if one of the big pet food companies also dispatched a congratulatory message.

Incidentally, Contessa eats a very simple diet: one can per day of kidney and tuna. Pat says Contessa likes kitty kibbles but it doesn't like her and she will vomit after she has sampled some of the other cat's meals.

Along with all the wonderful stories about her family, Pat also divulged a couple of amazing tips I'd like to pass on to you:

> With four cats and a dog and a ferret, Pat has no flea problem! Her answer? Borax powder, sprinkled around the carpet, in the corners of the rooms, in couch cushions.

> When a kitty makes the mistake of using the carpet or floor for a litter box, sprinkle orange peel in the area, and that area will be avoided in the future.

CONTESSA
AND SATAN

... Contessa, age 31, and her former housemate Satan, who lived to age 17.

CHAPTER 9

GROOMING

Coat

As your pet ages, grooming on a *regular* basis becomes more and more important. This is an excellent time to discover any lumps or bumps or a variety of unfriendly conditions that could become very serious in your pet's life. Recently, while brushing Pebbles I found a lump about the size of a nickel in her neck area. An examination by our Dr. Susan Nolte proved it to be nothing serious, and she simply extracted the liquid that was there.

Always remember to comb and brush gently, so as not to aggravate any arthritic pain that might be present. As the animal ages the skin can become much more dry, flaky and itchy; so the daily brushing is usually welcomed by your pet. It just *has* to feel better!

Toenails

Since your Senior is not experiencing as much running or extensive walking on surfaces that would normally keep the toenails from getting too long, you must keep a close check on the nails. If they are allowed to get too long they can cause pain. It is not too difficult to trim them yourself; you just need to be shown by a professional. A nail trimmer is a good investment, as regular trips to a vet or groomer just for nail care can be expensive. And while you're in the toenail area be sure to check all around the pads area for small pebbles or other foreign matter. You may very often find bits of dried feces material matted in the hair between the individual pads. These can be easily (but very carefully) cut out by a pair of small scissors.

Anal Area

While you're grooming and brushing also check the anal area for bits of fecal matter that could have stuck to the long hair. Again, it can be easily removed either by brushing or, where necessary, by cutting out the matted hair.

Mouth and Teeth

Special attention needs to be paid to the Senior's mouth and teeth, since tooth loss and serious gum infections become more common as pets age. Also, the spread of bacteria from the mouth into the pet's bloodstream by way of infections around the teeth is an even more serious risk to the Senior's health. Tumors of the mouth and gums also become increasingly likely in an older pet.

Believe it or not, even an older animal can be taught to accept your daily cleaning of its teeth! If you have done it all her life, all the better! Pebbles was past 15 when I started to clean hers. While actual brushing of the teeth with a toothbrush (*Never* use people toothpaste.) is far more effective, there is an alternative way. Available at your vet's office are treated gauze pads (C.E.T.®) that you simply wrap around your finger and gently rub over each tooth. (Be sure your fingernail is short, as you do not want to bruise a tender gum.) Also available from your vet is C.E.T. spray which you can spray onto small gauze pads to do the cleaning. If there is a severe tartar build-up, your vet may advise that the pet's teeth be cleaned professionally. This is expensive and the pet must be anesthetized during the procedure; so it would be to your advantage if you could convince your animal to let you do the cleaning a few times a week.

As good as Pebbles was about my cleaning her teeth, I just never could teach her to rinse and spit! (And, no, she never learned to floss either!)

Skin

In my search for knowledge about natural products for our pets, I learned about Aloe Vera Gel 90% pure for skin irritations. It has been most effective in a hair-loss condition on Pebbles' tail. Be sure, however, to check with your own veterinarian before giving it a try.

MANDY
AND
SAMMIE

... Corky's two best friends just before Pebbles came into her life. They lived to be 15 and 16.

Homeopathy Literature

Veterinary homeopathy is a big field and is becoming more popular and successful all the time. I am really intrigued by it and I know that it works. If there is no naturopathic physician or anyone who practices homeopathy in your area, you might want to write to the following firm for their brochure "Discover Homeopathy":

> Homeopathic Educational Services
> 2124 Kittredge Street
> Berkeley, CA 94704
> 415/649-0294, 800/359-9051

They offer some excellent books, among them Natural Health for Dogs and Cats, Homeopathic Treatment of Small Animals, and Homeopathic Remedies (for dogs and cats).

EXTRA T.L.C.

COMPASSION AND UNDERSTANDING

PATIENCE + PATIENCE + PATIENCE

WATCHFULNESS

CHAPTER 10

CLEANLINESS IS NEXT TO GODLINESS

Sleeping Areas

We all strive to keep our pets' sleeping areas clean always, but a little more attention is needed when they reach Senior status. Sometimes there may be a bit of urine leakage, fecal material, a trace of blood or flakes of dried skin. I whip up slip-covers out of sturdy cotton (two per bed) for each bed the pet uses. (If you're not a good whipper-upper, surely there's a friend who will help.) It's so simple to pop the soiled ones in the washer while you use the spare.

Food and Water Bowls

Your pet's food and water bowls must always be kept as clean as possible. As they grow older they are more susceptible to germs and to a variety of illnesses.

It's always been my practice to wash feeding bowls thoroughly after each meal. There are bound to be bacteria and who knows what other unfriendly critters accumulating in an un-washed bowl. How would you like to have each meal simply dumped into your previous meal's dish?

Just as your hands are always clean when you prepare the other family members' food, be sure to wash them when you prepare your animal's meals. And, clean hands are always a must when giving pills.

De-pooping The Yard

I'm sure I don't have to mention the importance of constant and frequent poop-scooping in the yards of dogs and outside cats. It's simply good hygienic practice. Also, a geriatric pet with poor eye-sight can accidentally step in it's own droppings. (It's not a whole bunch of fun cleaning THAT out of paw pads!)

Pooper-scooper-upper

One of the best investments I ever made was my "pooper-scooper." It allows you to pick up all those goodies without bending over, and then you simply drop them into a sturdy bag for deposit in the covered trash can in the yard. The scooper is made of heavy-duty plastic with metal hardware, so it should be long-lasting. (Cost is about $20.00.) The handle is 30" long making it a real joy to use, especially if you have a bad back.

Extra T.L.C.

Compassion and Understanding

Patience + Patience + Patience

Watchfulness

CHAPTER 11

LETTERS ...
DID WE GET LETTERS!

While compiling this book I received such wonderful letters and formed many new friendships, most of them by mail. I would dearly love to have met each and every dog and cat that I was told about!

One great letter-writer, Laurie Quinlan, made such a profound statement — one I will never forget: "Let's say that behind every good human being is a devoted animal." Laurie and her family's lives were certainly enriched by Su-Su, their 16-year-old cat, and also by Lady, their 10-year-old dog.

* * *

Two good, old buddies from Northern California, the Betties, wrote a marvelous letter. Did they have some great pets! One memorable story was about Sweetie, a Dachshund, who was ten or eleven when she developed a severe disc problem that required surgery. After the surgery they were told that Sweetie might never walk again. Betty O wasn't about to accept that diagnosis and began her own form of treatment; with a towel under Sweetie's mid-section, Betty would lift her up to assist her in walking so that she could go out to perform her daily functions;

she massaged the little dog's legs and back daily; and, in three month's time, Sweetie walked again! Betty O must have been doing something right, as Sweetie lived to age 18. Beautiful letter — I loved it!

* * *

I had such a good letter from Joyce and Ed Hay who breed and raise Chow-Chows in Portland. There is also a 17-year-old Siamese cat in that happy family.

One very important point brought up by Joyce, that I had planned to discuss at length in this book, was confusion in our Senior animals. Just imagine how confusing it must be to an older animal to begin to lose its sight, its hearing or, many times, both. There is no way the animal can possibly understand these frightening changes taking place. Worse still is the confusing and certainly embarrassing sudden loss of either bladder or bowel control, after many years of fastidious toilet habits.

* * *

May I repeat:

Extra T.L.C.
Compassion and Understanding
Patience + Patience + Patience
Watchfulness

I have heard people say of their pets, "My dog (or cat) must be getting senile, it is doing all these weird things." I DO NOT believe that animals become senile. I believe, instead, that many of the difficult physical changes that are taking place in their older bodies simply confuse them and create unusual behavior from time to time.

Another experience, from another dear old California buddy, was so movingly told that I could not possibly improve upon it:

I live in a hillside house in the Hollywood hills. There are vast expanses of undeveloped land in the area. Over the years, I have been visited by hungry raccoons seeking food handouts, observed coyotes moving surreptitiously through the under-brush above my house, and on other occasions watched deer nibbling tender leaves.

One day in 1980, I looked out the sliding glass door of my living room and saw a skinny, mangy-looking, flea-infested, black and white cat walking across my patio. Being a confirmed cat-lover, I hurried out with a bowl of milk. However, the moment that he saw me, the cat disappeared into the brush above my house. Obviously, he had been born out of wedlock in the wilds of the Hollywood hills, and forced at an early age to be responsible for his own survival, and two-legged humans did not seem to fit into the nature of things. He was what most people would call a "wild cat."

I bought some cat food, which I began leaving in the patio where he could see it. When he started showing up daily to eat what to him must have been a heaven-sent feast, I started standing where he could see me, but posed no immediate danger to him. As he got used to my presence, I gradually stood a little closer to his dish of food each day, until finally he was eating next to me. On that wonderful day (for both of us) I reached down and scratched him behind the ear, which was probably the first time in his life he had ever been touched by a human, and from that moment on he was mine, or vice versa! In all, this taming process had taken about four weeks.

Now, having few personal possessions of his own,

he decided after a quick inspection of my house that it would be most convenient to move in with me that very day. For the next ten years he was as close to being as loving and friendly a pet that I could ever have wanted. After getting rid of his fleas, the mites in his ears, and he settled down to about seven square meals a day, he rapidly gained weight and developed into a well groomed, happy, fat cat. However, for some strange reason, when he opened his mouth to 'meow' a little, thin squeak came out of this big, male cat, hence his name "Squeakie."

The one pleasure (for him) that I had to deny him, was to sleep with me. I tried it once and that was enough. That night he was so delighted to be sharing my bed with me, that although it was a king-sized bed, with plenty of room for the both of us, he chose to share my pillow with me, and proceeded to bathe my face and hair, and various body parts of his, for most of the night, thereby keeping us both awake until around two in the morning when I finally had to evict him from the bedroom. From that night on the bedroom door was closed in his disappointed face when I retired.

I never knew how old Squeakie was when he adopted me, but for ten years we were a happy pet and master (and that term is inter-changeable.) Then he developed an incurable liver infection and I had to have him put to sleep on New Year's Eve 1990-1991. It was not a joyful night for me.

I still see evidence of the raccoons nightly forag-ing, an occasional coyote, and the deer seem to be much more plentiful these days. And, I keep wishfully watching the patio, hoping some day to see another hungry "wild" cat, searching for food, and possibly a comfortable home.

Bob Forrest, dear friend, I have wept more than once over your beautiful letter. I pray with all my heart that you now have another loving critter in your life.

* * *

Charlie, a dear little mixed breed, was rescued by lucky Dorene Young and they've had 17 wonderful years together. When I first heard from Dorene and learned that Charlie was now deaf, I called her to tell her about Gingko Biloba and Silicea 6X; I certainly hope she was able to try it and that it proved helpful. While Charlie still has one naughty (but funny) habit of pulling the toilet tissue out into the hall, he showed such good manners in sending my Pebbles a birthday card on her 16th birthday!

CHARLIE

... this is Dorene Young's charmer, giving someone in Oregon a good plug at age 17.

* * *

More favorite friends from California wrote like Rocky Girl's folks, Leila Johnston and Virginia Green, whom I miss very much. Rocky Girl is an adorable Shih Tzu whom I've loved for several years. She's had some pretty "rocky" times in her life, but I'm told she is in the best health now at age 14 than she has been for the last four years.

About four years ago, Rocky Girl developed an unusual and serious skin condition. (It was diagnosed as Eurythema Multiforma.) After various explorations and treatments, my friends were referred to the Veterinary Medical Teaching Hospital at Davis, California (part of the University of California system). Luckily, they made contact with Dr. Feldman, the hospital's chief endocrinologist. Tests disclosed to Dr. Feldman that Rocky had a malignant tumor on one of her adrenal glands which was sending a message that produced an excess of cortisone. (You lucky Californians who live in the vicinity of this fabulous facility!)

Little Rocky Girl had surgery for the removal of the affected adrenal gland. She was also given cortisone in gradually decreasing amounts until the other adrenal gland came back to normal.

Rocky Girl saw Dr. Feldman periodically during the following year, so any possible spread of the cancer could be checked. She was then treated as a "normal dog." The skin condition was almost cleared up after the surgery; however some evidence of it still remained. This was treated successfully by the use of Nolvasan Shampoo with Conditioner.

As if Rocky Girl hadn't had more than her share, she also experienced an eye problem: lack of tear production. This was then treated with Cyclosporin drops prescribed by Leila and Virginia's regular vet.

* * *

My first introduction to Mara Nesbitt was a fine newspaper article in the Portland *Oregonian*, which I had saved long before I had ever thought of writing a book. I was so glad that I did, as it gave me the opportunity to speak with Mara, a delightful and very knowledgeable gal, whose best friend was a 13-year-old Australian Shepherd named Orion. Mara is a respected massage therapist in the Portland area. To prove once again the importance of grooming and touching our Senior pets, a lump was discovered on Orion's elbow while Mara was massaging her. It was diagnosed as cancer and was removed. Since the elbow is such an active joint, the healing process was slow, so Mara's vet taught her how to use saline wraps and soon Orion was on the road to recovery.

Lucky Orion (not only does she have Mara), she has had a best buddy, a 9-year-old German Shepherd/Beagle named Zoe with whom to share what sounds like a very good life.

I really like one of Mara Nesbitt's theories: "Touching is important to keeping a pet healthy."

While a Senior pet is experiencing some of these old-age-related confusions, it must be reassuring to have a loving, gentle stroke on the head, chest, or back from someone she loves and trusts implicitly. Mara believes that massaging a pet can help speed recovery from an injury, ease the pain of arthritis in older animals and, as with humans, provide simple relaxation.

* * *

Another simply super pet I met through the mail was Grammie, Peggy Coleman's fantastic and famous 25-year-old cat! She was given a 25th birthday party celebration at the Memorial Coliseum by the Lewis & Clark Longhair Cat Club, as a guest of their annual cat show!!! I understand from Peggy that Grammie was also featured in the May, 1990 Cat Fancier Magazine! Although I have pictures of this truly beautiful kitty, courtesy of Peggy, I have not met her yet. I do look forward to the opportunity to do so.

GRAMMIE

... this lovely lady is still enriching Peggy Coleman's life at age 25.

* * *

And then there was Bear! How I would have loved knowing that sweetheart! Bear was Black Labrador and Vislia, so he looked like a 3/4's-grown Lab. He lived the good life until age 12+ with Patricia Roux and her family. When Bear became pretty blind, he responded immediately to Patricia's "careful," if she felt he was in danger, or to her command "easy," if there was a chance that Bear was headed for trouble. Patricia said that Bear was a great communicator. As an example, there were a few times when Bear unavoidably had an "accident" in the house while the family was out. Bear would meet them at the door upon their return and let them know "there was a problem."

* * *

There was an interesting letter from a lady (wish I had her name and address) who voiced some interesting observations: "Older dogs and cats are wonderful," "They seem to need constant assurance that you still love and care for them," "Mature animals have much more character than younger ones." She went on to say that she felt older animals need never feel insecure because we love them more for themselves than for the "cutesy antics of younger ones."

* * *

I really enjoyed hearing from Marilyn Lewis down in California. Such wonderful animals she has had over the years like Lucy, a feisty cat member of the family who could probably have lived until age 20 had not cancer claimed her at 16-1/2 and Sweetheart, who surely sounded like one. Sweetheart was a great mix of Labrador and German Shorthair Pointer who had more than her share of old-age ailments before being gently put to sleep at age 14-1/2. She was quite instrumental in raising and training Chip, an Irish Setter who lived the good life with Marilyn until he was almost 14. Though these (and other) beloved pets are gone, they are not forgotten. Marilyn's current family now consists of three dogs and a cat.

Marilyn Lewis certainly thinks as I do; when our beloved animals are ready for Pet Heaven, we should immediately find new critters to love and cherish. Everyone ends up a winner!

Marilyn is also concerned, as am I, about what happens to old and elderly dogs and cats when the animals' owner passes away. It is not always easy to place these older animals in new homes. It is a topic we, as owners of elderly pets, should really think seriously about especially if we, ourselves, are Seniors.

* * *

I had a most touching letter from Lora of Portland. After more than her share of hard knocks in this life, she certainly deserved the love and devotion of Bam Bam. They really needed one another. Lora rescued Bam Bam after he had been literally abandoned by his irresponsible family. What really beautiful experiences they shared together. Bam Bam was 18 when Lora wrote me her beautiful letter — if they are not together still, I pray that Lora now has another "best friend" exactly as dear and loving as Bam Bam.

BAM BAM

JACKSON

... dear Bam Bam enriched Lora Coon's life for just over 18 years before going up to Pet Heaven. Her new best friend, Jackson, was adopted from the Humane Society, age 1-1/2.

* * *

I received such a sweet letter from a delightful young lady, Shannon Blount. Her kitty, Rocky, was 14 when he died of a heart attack. For such a young person, she certainly had some wise comments and observations.

* * *

It was such a delight to hear from Roxanne Miller and to learn of Cricket, a Chihuahua very small in stature but certainly grand in the personality department! How I would have loved to have seen the wrestling matches that went on between Cricket and his little friend, the orphaned raccoon! After many good, happy years in a loving family, Cricket departed this life at age 13.

* * *

What a truly lucky kitty Jobe is to have April Lackey caring for her! Poor Jobe has more than her share of ailments which require daily baths (for a bad skin condition) and daily injections for her allergies. She also has arthritis. This is just too much for one Siamese to have to endure at age 11. All the extensive daily care can become pretty arduous, I am sure, but as April says, "She's a fun cat to have around." And, April's closing statement pretty much says it all: "It's pretty inconvenient at times, but she's our little girl!"

* * *

I personally admire, salute, and thank each of you now giving the necessary, time-consuming and sometimes distasteful daily care that so many times is necessary for your animal's continued well-being. At times it must be exhausting, frustrating and most certainly expensive. But you are doing it, faithfully and lovingly, and for someone that is one of the most important members of your family — your dear critter.

I ADMIRE AND CONGRATULATE YOU ALL!

* * *

There is a real sweetheart who lives next door to me. Her name is Coco and she is an 11-year-old Seal Point Siamese with the bluest eyes you have ever seen on a critter! In spite of lots of trauma in Coco's life, which has included three relocations to new homes and once being trapped inside her burning home, she is a pretty well-adjusted and happy girl. But then, she lives with a pretty loving and caring family, Mary, Ed, Chris and Cody Walker, which must account for a lot of her present well-being.

CHAPTER 12

BREAKFAST OR DINNER
OR
THE HIGHLIGHTS OF
YOUR PET'S DAY!

Feeding Times

Except when I have had puppies or young dogs, I have always fed both breakfast and dinner, rather than one meal at the end of the day. (How would you like to go all day with an empty stomach?) I believe (as have my veterinarians) that this routine of feeding is easier on an animal's digestive system and bowel functions.

I believe that an older animal especially benefits from two small meals rather than one large meal at the end of the day.

For the past several months Pebbles (now past 16) hasn't been too excited about breakfast, no prancing around or real interest, though she eats and seems always to enjoy it. But dinner is another matter! She's been up several hours and the early morning kinks and pains have subsided. As I start to fix her dinner, there is definite interest and desire, and when I carry her bowl from the kitchen into the utility room where she is fed, she prances around like a youngster. (One of the reasons that I purchased the heavy plastic runners was so she wouldn't slip and fall, possibly causing an injury.)

Bench Feeding

Many years ago, since Pebbles is such a large dog, I began "bench feeding." For those of you not familiar with the term, this is the offering of the animal's food and water a good distance up from the floor level. For a large animal, it constitutes much less strain on the neck and back not to have to bend down to floor level to eat or drink. Plus food and water have an easier trip down the throat. Pebbles' bowls are in a metal container 12" from the floor.

Bench feeding is not only ideal for older pets with arthritis or hip dysplasia, but the concept also reduces gulping of the food and air intake. I am of the opinion that even medium- sized dogs would benefit from bench feeding, at a height commensurate with their size.

For a long time, before I invested in one of the bench feeding units, I used to pull out a little-used, low, kitchen drawer, set a plastic tray on it and place Pebbles' food and water bowls there. Worked just fine.

Pill Giving

I have been fortunate in that all my animals have taken pill medication very easily, even by mouth. I guess I've just been lucky in that regard, as I hear horror stories from friends who have a terrible time getting pills down an uncooperative dog or cat. At present, Pebbles gets six pills, at breakfast and dinner, which I simply tuck into the kibble. It is very rarely that she leaves one in the bowl. If she does (and your animal must take the prescribed dosage of any medication in order for it to be effective), I simply open her mouth with my left thumb and forefinger and pop the neglected pill to the rear of her throat. I immediately close her mouth and gently stroke her neck to promote swallowing.

In an earlier chapter I told of adding chicken to Pebbles' kibble to promote weight gain. Once her weight was back to normal it was sad to deny her this treat, as she loves chicken. Since I can't be a complete ogre, I still add just a dash (a scant two tablespoons) of unsalted chicken broth to her kibble. By vigorously shaking the bowl, all the kibble gets a slight coating, but not enough to soften it.

Water

Since we, as companions of Seniors, must always do all that we possibly can to guard them against infection, we can't overlook the possible danger of a bowl of water that has been sitting all night. I have always changed my animals' water first thing in the morning before they have a chance to have even one lap. In addition, it's a good idea to let the water run from the tap for a few seconds in the morning to flush out any impurities that may be sitting in the pipes. (I have always offered fresh water morning, noon and dinner-time.)

I have a close friend whose large dog suffers from arthritis and she is of the opinion that distilled water is very beneficial for the condition. It's something you may wish to discuss with your veterinarian.

Sugar

If you don't know about sugar and your animals, you certainly should. It is very definitely a no-no-no. That goes for candy, ice-cream, cookies or any product containing sugar.

Mid-day Outing

As my two miniature poodles aged (Pebbles' predecessors), I was still a working person. I didn't want them to have to be in the house the whole time I was at the office. I was fortunate enough to have a trusted neighbor child who could come to the house in the middle of the day, let them out and give them fresh water. I was more fortunate than most, as I had all the wonderful Locke kids to do my dog-sitting; as one outgrew the job, I had the next in line to depend on!

BONUS

When you feed any top-quality dog or cat food, you will find smaller BM's to clean up, good news in anyone's back yard or litter box!

EXTRA T.L.C.
COMPASSION AND UNDERSTANDING
PATIENCE + PATIENCE + PATIENCE
WATCHFULNESS

CHAPTER 13

FROM ANAL SACS TO ZINGERS

Sleeping Late

About a month before Pebbles' 16th birthday, she began sleeping in until about 10:00AM. The first time it happened I was terrified and kept tip-toeing into the bedroom to make sure she was still breathing. Most of the time, she would get up at about 7:30 when I got up to make my tea. After a trip outside she would join me as I went back to bed to read for half an hour. Thank God for retirement — we can just make our own hours. On the many mornings when she doesn't hear me get up for good, at around 8:30, I just try to be very quiet. I don't do the dishes or make any unnecessary noise to awaken her. After all, she deserves the right, along with all of us old Seniors, to sleep just as late as she pleases!

Barking, But Why?

From about age 15, Pebbles developed a strange little habit: when I would go out the front door to water the plants or go out to the mail box, she would bark and become quite agitated, even though she could see me through all the windows in the living room. The barking would also occur when visiting guests were ready to leave by the front door, as she must have assumed that I was going to leave too. Again, this was a sad display of insecurity as felt by an elderly animal.

As I stated earlier, it will be most gratifying to me if I can, by means of this book, instill in everyone reading it the importance of

EXTRA T.L.C.

COMPASSION AND UNDERSTANDING

PATIENCE + PATIENCE + PATIENCE

WATCHFULNESS

Equally as important to your dear Senior's well-being is ... Attentiveness

Be constantly aware of any significant changes in your animal: bowel elimination, urine elimination, appetite changes, skin abnormalities, irritability, excessive water consumption. Try always to remember that small problems in an older animal can all too quickly become big ones. As they grow older their ability to fight disease and infections of all kinds diminishes greatly. Better to make a visit to your vet with just a tiny skin growth, than to wait until it develops into something really serious and difficult to treat or cure. Here is where the little notebook comes in very handy; jot down everything out of the ordinary, so that you have accurate facts to present to your vet.

An Ounce Of Prevention

Just as all of us should have a yearly physical examination, with all pertinent lab tests, so should our Senior pets. The old adage, "An ounce of prevention is worth a pound of cure" could not be more true when it comes to our aging animals. Your own vet will give you good direction when it comes to the frequency of your individual pet's preventative visits.

Children And Older Pets

In another section I have mentioned children present at social gatherings and the precautions to take with your older or elderly pet. The same precautions and common sense should prevail at all times when there are young children in the household. They must be made aware that their dearly loved pet may not be as receptive to lots of hugging and rough playing now. It's certainly not that their animal loves them any less, it's just that some loving and hugging can hurt! An arthritic back is painful and a well-meaning but too enthusiastic hug could result in a nip from an older dog or a scratched hand from an otherwise docile kitty. Try to explain to very young children that the older pets must be treated so very gently, just as they would treat an elderly human member of the family. If the compassion and understanding of the situation just is not there, it might be best to leave the care of the pet to an adult family member. Remember, try to make your animal's life as stress-free as is humanly possible. The happier she is, the longer she is going to live!

Fourth of July

From the first Fourth of July with Pebbles when I learned how terrified she was of firecrackers, I never left my home on that date again. When she was much younger I used to get tranquilizers from our California vet; however, I don't believe they are good for our older pets. So now, each year, I just put some lovely, soothing music on the radios in the bedroom, the kitchen, and perhaps one other room or the patio. I have the volume high enough so that the animal can really hear it well, and hopefully all outside sounds of those idiots with the illegal firecrackers won't be heard. If the neighbors are disturbed, so be it. More important is that your animal is more comfortable and can make it through that traumatic day. Spend lots of time touching and speaking soothingly to the animal and do not leave her alone. If your neighborhood has more than it's share of idiots with unusually loud fireworks, and your pet likes to ride in the car, that might be the day for a long, leisurely drive. (Don't forget the leash, water and paper towels!)

Eyes - Cataracts

Since the eyes of our pets can give us many clues as to possible abnormalities or on-coming illnesses, it would be wise to discuss this with your veterinarian and ask him to give you a list of the danger signs for which you should look.

Cataracts are so common in our older dogs and cats. I have known many elderly animals with pronounced cataracts and it doesn't seem to slow them down too much. As long as they are not moved to a new home they seem to function very well, since they have just about everything memorized in the digs they've lived in for so long. Cataract surgery is quite common and many times very successful in older animals. Still, your vet must decide if it is for you and your Senior. Pebbles has cataracts; yet while I see evidence of her failing sight, she can still spot one tiny kibble dropped on the kitchen floor when I point to it! Unless my vet advised me that there was a real medical emergency connected with her eyes, I would not subject her to cataract surgery at her age of 16.

Anal Sacs

Just one more of the joys of growing old! When people observe their Senior dragging her rear on the ground or the carpet, they often think it is caused by worms in the animal.

Not so, usually. It can possibly be that the anal glands are filled and need to be expressed. This is generally something that your vet must do; however, it may be that he can teach you how. Don't let it go unattended, as it can be painful and there is a very good possibility that the anal sacs can become infected causing real problems.

Clothing

It wasn't until our move to beautiful Oregon (with all its beautiful rain) that I gave much thought to any kind of coat for Pebbles. During our first winter here, I changed my mind and decided she could benefit from some protection when she had to go "out" in the pouring rain. You would be surprised how difficult it is to find a really smashing raincoat for a 50-pound dog! (Also, these items of apparel are quite expensive.)

I borrowed a dog coat from a very petite neighbor Poodle, cut a pattern and purchased some water-proof fabric (similar to the yellow 'slickers' you see). I first practiced on some old fabric. After a few trials and many errors, I came up with a pretty acceptable coat for Pebbles, one that would definitely keep her dry on those many trips to the back yard. She accepted the idea quite well, especially after about the second trip out in a down-pour, since she has never enjoyed getting really wet. I am presently in the process of constructing some suitable rain boots, since she also hates having her feet wet! There are boots for large dogs on the market, but again, they are quite expensive and I don't see why I can't come up with a solution. In the meantime, I still towel-dry her feet when she comes in from outside. It's important. It's not healthful for an animal to lie around with wet, cold feet. Also there could be accumulated mud between the pads that needs to be removed. It just takes a few minutes and it makes the animal so much more comfortable.

Pebbles and Snow

The first time Pebbles saw snow was quite a sight to behold! Our first winter in Oregon we had 4" just before Christmas. I have a beautiful picture of her foot prints in the snow on the deck. As she stepped out, she would lift one paw, then another and shake it, like a cat when it gets its feet wet. She got used to it in a hurry though, as we had the snow for several days. Here again will be an excellent time to use the boots, since a fall on an icy surface could prove dangerous and result in a painful injury.

Nose

Discharges from the nose should alert you to a potential disease condition. A clear discharge may indicate allergies or viral infections. Green mucoid discharge indicates a bacterial infection. (Thank you, Dr. Goodman.)

Ears

Ear problems are most common. Look for any discharge, redness, or odor from the ear canal. Constant head shaking or scratching at the ears are other signs of otitis or ear infections. Some breeds actually grow hair in their ear canals and require it to be plucked on a regular basis. (Thank you again, Doctor Goodman.)

CHAPTER 14

GUIDE DOGS
FOR THE BLIND, INC.

One of the organizations nearest and dearest to my heart is Guide Dogs, located in San Rafael, California, and known and revered throughout the country. I have been a member for years.

If you are vacationing in or near Northern California, it will be one of the highlights of your trip if you can arrange to be there at graduation time. They are held monthly. Not only are these magnificent dogs presented to blind people absolutely free of charge, but when you hear some of the stories of the graduates of how these dogs have enhanced their independence, you feel you will never again complain about any inconvenience in your own life.

First, the young puppies are "puppy-tested" by a dedicated group of people who check their potential. Next, the puppies are placed in the homes of volunteer puppy raisers, usually young 4-H members who rear and love the pups for 15 months. And, heart-breaking as it may be, these young people then give up the puppies to the school for their extensive training as future Guide Dogs for their new masters. More months of hard work by dedicated trainers follow. Finally, the dogs are introduced to their future masters and another month of hard training takes place between dog and master. Graduation day is something you will never forget, if you are ever fortunate enough to attend one. At a Guide Dogs graduation the young 4-H member who has raised the puppy for 15 months is introduced and in a very touching, brief ceremony, presents the now beautifully trained Guide Dog to the new master. There are usually about 16 to 24 dog/owner teams at each graduation. I can't remember how many graduations I have attended, but I do remember that none were ever tear-free.

Since there is no charge to the blind person for the month-long stay at the School, for the training or for the magnificent animal who will become her/his new lease on life, Guide Dogs For The Blind, Inc. depends on donations from the public for its existence. And, you can become a member, no matter where you live!

Guide Dogs For The Blind, Inc.
Post Office Box 151200
San Rafael, CA 94915-1200

Donations range from very nominal amounts to as size-able a figure as you wish to make. For any size donation, you will receive the monthly newsletter which contains information about school activities on up-coming fund-raising events, success letters from and articles about graduates, informative articles by the resident veterinarian, and lots of gorgeous pictures of various Guide Dogs. In mid-summer, the newsletter prints a picture of the next Christmas card, along with an order blank and instructions for ordering. They are stunning cards and very reasonably priced. All proceeds from their sale benefit Guide Dogs.

My dearest connection to Guide Dogs was Hula. Many years ago I was fortunate enough to become Hula's "mom." Since the Guide Dogs organization wanted their breeding stock to live in family environments, I was lucky enough to qualify to have Hula as my beloved family pet when she was not needed at the school.

When she was needed for breeding purposes, I returned her to Guide Dogs. She was back home with us during her pregnancy and when the time came for her to have her litter, she was returned to Guide Dogs. When the babies were weaned, Hula once again came home to us.

This magnificent German Shepherd was one of the most memorable animals I have ever lived with. She was gentle, loving, protective, intelligent beyond words, and in every way a joy to know and love. She had a fantastic record in the puppies she produced; they all "made the grade," and several who did not become Guide Dogs themselves, were so outstanding they were put into the Guide Dogs breeding program.

My beloved Hula lived just past 12 years. She developed some tumors of the breasts, along with a few other complications, and was put gently to sleep. I still have her chain collar, her number was B-12.

HULA

... Corky's beloved dog, however, she also belonged to Guide Dogs For the Blind, Inc., as she was one of their top brood bitches many years ago. Hula lived to just past 12 years.

* * *

In each Guide Dogs News there will be an article by Craig Dietrich, DVM, long-time veterinarian for Guide Dogs For The Blind. His advice is always sound and I have saved many of his articles. With permission the following article from Dr. Dietrich's column, "Pointers From the Veterinarian" is reproduced for your information.

Care For A Common Ailment

Experienced veterinarians are generally able to predict the nature of certain phone calls based on when the call is made. For example, early morning calls frequently concern a dog that has had diarrhea all night. A similar call often comes late Friday afternoon. This one usually refers to a dog that has had diarrhea for one or two days. The dog has diarrhea every time it eats and this caller, like the first one, wants to know how to stop the problem and what to feed the dog.

In both instances we have acute cases of simple diarrhea, the cause of which can be difficult to uncover. The dog may have ingested garbage, eaten food too rich for its digestion — such as human food — or simply overindulged in dog food. Bacteria or an infectious virus may also be the culprit.

Regardless of the cause, the treatment is the same. The single best thing to feed the dog for the 24 to 48 hour period following a sudden diarrhea attack is absolutely nothing! By abstaining from food the cells in the intestinal tract are given a chance to repair and rebuild without having to do any additional work when food passes through. The dog can be allowed water at normal watering times as long as it isn't vomiting.

Many anti-diarrhea products are available over the counter, but in most cases they are not necessary. Pepto-Bismol® is as helpful as any of these products and can be given at the adult dosage for two to three days. Some dogs accept the flavor readily, while with others it will help to put the liquid medication in a small turkey baster first. Put the tip of the turkey baster in the corner of the dog's mouth and gently squeeze the medication over the tongue. As an alternative, Kaopectate® or Pepto-Bismol® tablets may be given at the human dosage for two to three days.

The final important step in treating diarrhea is beginning to feed your dog again. Start with a bland diet of four parts boiled white rice to one part boiled chicken or cooked ground beef with *all* grease removed. Feed one to two cups of this mixture three to four times a day for one to two days. Gradually, over the next four to five days, resume the normal diet for the dog.

Once back to a normal diet, don't feel sorry for the dog because of its seemingly monotonous diet and begin adding flavor enhancers. By adding such tidbits, you could create the problem once again.

Finally, if you feel that more is wrong than an attack of simple diarrhea or if the diarrhea does not abate after the above course of treatment, do not hesitate to contact your own veterinarian immediately. If the doctor wants to see the dog, be sure to take a fresh stool sample along.

Craig Dietrich, DVM
(Reprinted from GUIDE DOG NEWS,
Vol. 37, No.1, Spring 1987.)

CHAPTER 15

OLD DOG — OLD TRICK

Litter Boxes -- For Dogs ⁇⁇⁇

Why not? I would not be at all surprised if you could teach your older dog to use one. In inclement weather it could be a real blessing! Our older dogs are not senile; they are every bit as intelligent as they once were. Sure, they've slowed down in many ways, but most will still respond to all the commands they were taught when they were young. And, since a dog is so terribly eager to please its master, I wouldn't be surprised to see this new "trick" successfully taught. Moreover, if your dog is one who especially does not like going out in the rain, she might just love your ingenious new idea!

For a large animal it might be necessary to attach two litter boxes together. And, naturally, you will keep the canine litter box just as clean and fresh as you do those for the feline members of the family.

(Sudden Thought!) How about using an automobile drip pan, the metal tray that people place under their cars? It's about 1/2" deep and certainly large enough. You will not be needing much litter material or a very deep pan since a dog would not be following the cat's burying principle.

The more I think about the idea, the better I like it and the more eager I am to give it a good try. The benefits abound: no more wet, muddy and cold feet; no soaked fur; and best of all, the elimination of countless opportunities for your animal to catch a cold or other respiratory ailments.

I know that old dogs can be taught new tricks; Pebbles learned two after the age of 15!

Treats

I've always used the good, old standard dog biscuits as dessert, as rewards, and as a special treat. Since it's very important to eliminate salt from our older animal's diet, a good and nutritious substitute would be a pet vitamin, such as Pet Tabs® Plus. These are most important in their diet and animals love them. Pebbles made the switch very easily. (Be sure to check with your own vet for the vitamin supplement that he recommends.)

Food — Read Labels

We've all tried to give the very best food that we can to our animals all their lives. Now that they are Seniors, it is even more important that they have the very finest that is available. Although it can be a strain on the old budget, the best rule of thumb is to buy the most expensive you can afford, because that is usually the most nutritionally perfect for your animal. By keeping your Senior nutritionally healthy, you will very probably cut down on your veterinary bills. Your vet is your best source of information for what you should be feeding your pet.

Get in the habit of reading dog and cat food labels. There are quite a few ingredients in many of them that you *don't* want to put in those precious tummies; there are some that are downright dangerous to your animal's health! Again, your own vet can supply you with this very vital information. Keep in mind that our older animals should have a diet that is low in salt, protein and calories.

Old Dog — Old Trick

One evening not too long ago, I was upset that Pebbles had not been walked for a couple of days because it had been raining steadily. I suddenly remembered something that we used to do in California for the same reason (when we had rain, that is). I had taught her to "find the ball." I would have her stay in the kitchen while I hid a tennis ball somewhere in the living room, under a table, behind a cushion, in a plant stand. She could see me from the kitchen as I circled the entire room, deciding where to hide the ball. Then I would call her out to "find the ball." Sometimes it would take ten minutes, but it was always found. I would then give the command "go hide your eyes," and back into the kitchen she would go. The ball was hidden again, and again found. She loved this game and I felt she was getting a bit of exercise in spite of the weather.

On more than one occasion I would see her locate the ball, but move on to search elsewhere, as if she were thinking "the old girl loves this game so much, guess I'll just try to prolong it a bit for her."

We had not played our game for over four years, yet when I got out a ball and asked if she wanted to "find the ball?," she was elated! I had to take her to this new kitchen and tell her that this was where she was to stay and hide her eyes. I then proceeded to the living room to hide the ball. This time Pebbles moved a bit slower and took a bit longer getting her front paws up on the various pieces of furniture to search behind the cushions, but she thoroughly enjoyed our old rainy day game. Instead of the seven or eight times that we used to go through the whole routine, I have cut it down to two or three each session because of her arthritic back. So, you see, older animals are not senile — they've just slowed down a bit.

Pet-Sitting

We all enjoy caring for friend's and neighbor's pets while the owners are away. The favor can then be reciprocated ensuring to all involved that their animals are going to be properly cared for when they are away. Should there be more than one person involved in the animal's care, be certain that there is good communication between the two.

A most disturbing event took place recently at the home of dear friends who were caring for the next-door love, Danny. Through lack of communication, what had started out to be a lovely dinner party turned into an evening of anxiety and frustration. My hostess was feeding Danny each day after she returned from work. On this particular evening, when she went to give him his dinner, he was not there. You can well imagine the anguish we all went through for a few long, long hours. It so happened that another neighbor had taken Danny out for a walk but had not communicated this to the other care-giver. Everything turned out all right — Danny had his walk and his dinner — but there were four of us who developed a few more gray hairs that we didn't need or want.

The point of this story is that if there are more than two people acting as care-givers to pets, be sure that each has the other's address and phone number, and that they will coordinate the activities involving the animals.

Specimens To Vet

When your animals are ill and the vet asks you to bring in a fecal or urine sample, don't panic, for it's not as difficult as you might think. With your kitty, simply raid the litter box. With your dog, have a wide-neck container (a cottage cheese tub works well) in your hand as you let her out the first time in the morning. Follow closely behind the pet and, as she is ready to "squat," simply slip the container under her bottom. Transfer the urine you have collected to a small jar with a tightly fitting lid. After you've picked up a small fecal sample, place that in another small jar with a lid. If your vet has a good sense of humor (as most do) you might want to tie a colorful bow on each before presenting them to him.

Hearing Loss

If your hearing-impaired Senior is trotting down the hall trying to find you, and you know she won't hear you if you call, try stomping on the floor a few times. Many times the vibrations will turn her around towards you.

Speaking of hearing loss AND improvement! I am still seeing evidences of Pebbles' greatly improved hearing. One recent morning as I finished my reading in bed, I put the book on the night table and the metal book mark fell out, making a slight noise. The Princess was still asleep, but she immediately raised her head at the sound! It is said it's the little things in life that count the most — how true that is! (Please see "Gingko Biloba," Chapter 3, for treatment of hearing loss.)

Diet and Cancer

A couple of years ago when I began to realize I had a four-legged Senior in my midst, I tried to read and to learn whatever I could about older dogs. One close veterinarian friend told me quite a bit about cancer in dogs. He was of the opinion that poor nutrition can actually be the cause of cancer in our animals. Further, that if you have a happy, well-adjusted dog, one who has a minimum of stress in it's life, the chances of the dog contracting cancer are greatly lessened. I've never forgotten his words and try to live by them faithfully. This seems a very small price to pay in order to lessen the chances of such a deadly disease.

Extra T.L.C.
Compassion and Understanding
Patience + Patience + Patience
Watchfulness

CHAPTER 16

A LITTLE BIT
OF EVERYTHING

Temperature

Hopefully, everyone reading this book knows how to take her dog or cat's temperature. It's really quite simple and most pets will accept the procedure without too much complaint. Again, have your vet show you how. Purchase a thermometer for your pet's use exclusively and mark it accordingly. Normal temperature for a dog is 101.5 to 102.5; for a cat it is the same. If your Senior has a health emergency, it will be valuable to your vet if you can tell him the animal's temperature on the first phone call.

Pet Notebook

Another valuable tool for you, but especially for your vet, is a small loose-leaf notebook. Keep a record of abnormalities in your Senior's day (or night), along with time, duration, severity, and anything pertinent to the situation. Then, when a visit to the vet is necessary, take your little book of helpful information along. Lacking one of those fantastic memories for every little detail I have always used the "daily record" method of keeping track of my animal's health as she aged.

The little notebook is also invaluable in keeping track of your animal's medications. Note the date and dosage of each medication; should you have been instructed by your vet to either increase or decrease the dosage after a certain period of time, enter these dates and changes also. This will help you be certain that the proper medications will always be administered.

Should a medication be prescribed as "one tablet, three times per day," and you inadvertently skip one of the dosages, do not double up on the next dosage unless you have checked this with your vet. In addition, if an animal who has been ill suddenly seems to be quite well again before all the prescribed medication has been given, do not simply discontinue the medication; check with your vet, as chances are that he had intended that the entire prescription be given to the animal.

Golden Seal

Once after a camping trip, Pebbles developed a very bad "hot spot" about the size of a quarter just under her chin. I treated it for several days with a well-known and good veterinary salve but it just was not healing. I made a visit to a local health food store inquiring if they could suggest any remedy. I was told to use "Golden Seal" in powder form. (This is a "human" remedy, simply wonderful if taken at the on-set of a cold.) I sprinkled about one-half a capsule on the affected area and the next day the area, once very red and raw, had started to dry up. I continued sprinkling Golden Seal on the hot spot, three times a day for two more days. Very shortly thereafter, the spot was healed and the hair on Pebbles' neck began to grow back. Golden Seal is an herb which was discovered by Native Americans. Again, check with Uncle Doctor before using it on your animal.

Introducing New Puppy Or Kitten

There has always been much discussion, pro and con, on the practice of bringing a new puppy or kitten into a family with a Senior animal. One argument "for" is that the new family member is going to give a new lease on life to the older pet and to allow her to live longer. I'm sure in many instances this practice is successful.

Personally, I don't feel that this is a good idea. First, your Senior is bound to be pretty confused by this arrangement: "I've been their loyal and loving companion for all these years. Why would they suddenly bring a young up-start into MY home?"

Secondly, a lot of your time is now taken up seeing to the needs and comforts of your elderly animal. How is there going to be a lot of time for training and raising a new, young animal, too?

The youngster is going to want to run and play with an almost unending amount of energy. Your elderly pet is probably not up to this type of exertion, and too much hard play and activity could actually do some damage. Remember, her heart and lungs are just not as strong and resilient as they once were. Also, if there is an arthritic condition, it is bound to be aggravated.

I firmly believe that introducing another animal (young or adult) into the household will be the cause of a lot of stress in your Senior. And, we all should be very aware of trying to eliminate as much stress as possible in our Senior's lives.

Speaking from my own experience with several elderly animals, I have always found that they tend to become more possessive and dependent as they age. I just know that none of them would ever have wanted to share me or their home with a new animal.

Just try to always remember — the geriatric dog or cat should have quiet, limited activity, and NO stress.

Stress

It was not until starting to compile this book that I was aware of stress in younger animals, too. My dear computer guru Pat LeSuer, educated me on this subject. Each time an animal of any age is moved from one home to another it can be a stressful experience, and must be acknowledged and treated as such.

EXTRA T.L.C.

COMPASSION AND UNDERSTANDING

PATIENCE + PATIENCE + PATIENCE

WATCHFULNESS

Vaccinations

Just because our animals are getting older is no reason to become lax about their yearly booster vaccinations! They may have much less contact with other animals or they may be leading a much less strenuous life; however, they still need their boosters regularly. Your veterinarian will always advise you what booster is needed and when. Also, you will not be able to renew an animal's license if vaccinations are not regularly updated.

Water

Be sure that plenty of cool water is always available, inside and outside. In extremely hot weather you should change it a few times a day so that it is always cool and refreshing. Adding a few ice cubes to the water bowl helps keep it cooler.

On those rare nights when the temperature in the house stays quite warm, you might want to move the animal's bed close to a screened window, but never to a spot where she might be in a draft.

First Aid Kit

I've always assembled first aid kits for my animals; a sturdy little carton with a tight fitting lid works just fine. If you're going on a vacation trip, pop it right in the trunk along with the luggage. Your vet is your best source of information for what your kit should contain for your own particular animal. This is generally what mine contained: [Dog or cat]

thermometer	tweezers
package of sterile	Golden Seal capsules
gauze pads	bandage scissors
hydrogen peroxide	first aid ointment
(small, tightly	(NeoSporin
capped bottle)	or Mycitracin)
rolls of gauze	small container of
(narrow & wide)	Pepto Bismol®
aspirin (tightly capped)	

On a little card taped to the top of the carton note the dates of expiration for any of the products that have a shelf life. Rotate these items as needed.

When you plan to travel with your animal, PLEASE don't forget her prescription medications, and it couldn't hurt to have a copy of your vet's prescription, along with his phone number, in case the prescription needs to be refilled away from home.

(Note: Keep in mind that aspirin is toxic to our cats — be sure to check with your vet before using any similar product.)

Teeth

When we live with Senior animals, we must do everything we can to protect their teeth. This is one more reason why I have always fed my animals Hill's® Science Diet® products as apposed to soft, mushy or "people" food. The latter allows tooth surfaces to become coated with putrefying food, thus inviting the formation of plaque.

While it may be very difficult to ignore those pleading eyes that silently, but so intently, beseech you for just a bite of that roast chicken or just a taste of those mashed potatoes, be brave and stick to the Senior Maintenance or Canine Senior or Feline Senior (all made by Hill's®), or any other top quality pet food.

Yearly Exams

And, another reminder: a regular, yearly examination by your vet after your animal is between the ages of five and seven is so very important. This will do much to ensure that your best friend will reach healthy Senior status.

Incontinence

In researching the fascinating subject of homeopathy and in speaking with a few veterinarian friends, I learned that incontinence is very successfully treated by *causticum*, which is a preparation of sulfuric acid. Many feel that it is a far superior medication to DES, which can produce many side effects. Discuss the product with your vet. Hopefully, it will solve the problems you might be having with this ailment.

Fourth of July

Recently, in a little round-table discussion of how we endeavor to protect our animals from the horrors of the Fourth of July, someone mentioned phosphorus. The results achieved by those who had tried it were amazing. I would wholeheartedly suggest that you discuss the product with your vet and a homeopathic or naturopathic physician. I am really very impressed with the homeopathic and naturopathic professionals that I have met and talked with since starting this book; they have all been "people doctors," but they have all been such caring and concerned individuals. It did not matter to them that my inquiries were with regard to a beloved critter and not a human patient. Their genuine concern about my problems and their desire to be of assistance in any way possible was always so evident. I will be eternally grateful to Rick Marinelli, N.D. both for the restoration of my dog's hearing and for the alleviation of pain caused by her arthritis.

Choke Chains

It is amazing to me the number of people who are not aware of the dangers of a choke chain collar. THEY CAN KILL! This type of collar must be used ONLY when walking or training your animal. When the walk or the training session is completed, replace the collar *immediately* with the animal's regular collar.

More Stress

It was not until beginning this book and doing much research into topics such as stress that I ever realized just how severe it can be in our animals' lives.

Shortly after Pebbles' and my move to Oregon in 1989 she chewed incessantly on her tail; that magnificent, big, golden tail was almost hairless on the underneath side. I had attributed it to the flea problem we were having and had endeavored to treat the problem accordingly. It was several months before the condition cleared up and the hair began to grow back.

And, I now realize that it was also stress that caused her to follow me from room to room constantly. (After over two years she still does it a great deal of the time.) My poor beloved dog — little did I know the stress to which I had subjected her.

Pebbles was 13 at the time of our move, but I just never realized that I had an elderly animal! There never seemed to be any aging signs until Pebbles was past 15.

Replacement Surgery

I was so happy to read recently of very successful hip replacement surgery on a lovely Golden Retriever suffering from severe hip dysplasia. After two days the dog was walking, and in two weeks he was no longer limping! Beautiful!

EXTRA T.L.C.

COMPASSION AND UNDERSTANDING

PATIENCE + PATIENCE + PATIENCE

WATCHFULNESS

CHAPTER 17

OBESITY
(THE DIRTY WORD)

The above is a *dirty word*. It is a true health hazard in any of our pets, but even more so in our Senior pets, as it *does* shorten their lives. So, you're not doing your animal a favor by offering extra treats or dinner left-overs.

I'm a firm believer, as is every veterinarian I've ever known, in absolutely no deviation from your Senior's regularly pre-scribed diet, no matter how convincing those sad, begging, oh-I'm-really-starving eyes can be.

When we, as owners, have available completely nutritious, balanced meals that a lot of brilliant people spend their lives per-fecting, why would we possibly want to offer anything else to our best friends?

I had always given Pebbles a large dog biscuit as desert after her dinner. She also got a half biscuit as a "mid-night" snack when we went to bed after the last "out." Recently, Dr. Goodman suggested that I cut back on this practice, due to the amount of salt she was getting. I've replaced dessert and the late-night snack with vitamin tablets. Pebbles is just as happy, judging from the speedy manner in which the tablets disappear.

Not only is obesity extremely detrimental to your Senior's

heart, liver and kidneys, but that extra weight being carried around is also definitely adding to the pain caused by arthritis. In addition, obesity aggravates constipation, and the obese dog or cat is more prone to developing diabetes.

A pretty good way to tell if dear Senior is over-weight is to see if you can feel her ribs. You should be able to. Again, your personal vet is the one to advise you when your pet is too heavy.

EXTRA T.L.C.
COMPASSION AND UNDERSTANDING
PATIENCE + PATIENCE + PATIENCE
WATCHFULNESS

CHAPTER 18

HERE,
KITTY, KITTY

Having owned only two cats in my lifetime (and neither of them very old), I have had to rely quite a bit on library research and some invaluable input from my veterinary friends for much of the kitty material for this book. Also, the many new friends who responded to my request to share their experiences with their beloved felines helped me greatly. Fortunately, so many of the afflictions, symptoms and treatments that are noted herein as pertaining to canines can also relate to felines.

After reliving with friends so many marvelous, sad, funny and unbelievable accounts of living with cats, I felt maybe I've missed a lot in not having a kitty in residence along with all the dogs I've had … Perhaps next time …

'Cricket'

Dear Cricket is the sweetheart that appears on the cover of this book, and she held a very special place in my heart for the all-too-short time that I knew her.

Our first meeting did not start out too happily since I had been told by Bea Clements and Annette Woods, "Oh, she won't come to you — she never goes to strangers." I was pretty disappointed, as here was one sweet kitty I would have liked to be my friend. Cricket was past 16 at this time.

Shortly after I arrived at Bea and Annette's home, we sat down at the table for one of Bea's fabulous lasagna dinners. (Cricket had disappeared some place shortly after setting eyes on me.) About fifteen minutes into our sumptuous meal there was a little sound, a little pressure in my lap area, and a little grey cat curled up on my dinner napkin! I tried to act very nonchalant and didn't speak to her or touch her. I had a dinner companion for the remainder of the meal and a good buddy from then on.

Poor little Cricket had more than her share of kitty ailments and she was to spend a good deal of time at the hospital under the loving care of Dr. J. Scott Davis of Portland, until she was gently put to sleep at 17-1/2 years. I grieved right along with Bea and Annette at their loss of one who was a dear little friend for so many years.

One of my most treasured pictures in "The Critters Room" (see Chapter 32 on Wolves) is a 20" x 30" picture of Cricket out in the spectacular garden of my two friends. They had had it enlarged and framed for me for Christmas one year.

'Raskal'

When Raskal was 15 she suffered from renal failure. The first veterinarian that her best friend and companion, Robin Sparks of Portland, took her to left much to be desired. He seemed to be of the opinion that there was not much to be done for a 15-year-old cat who was quite ill, so why not just let her go? This was not acceptable to Robin, and luckily, she found Dr. Laird Goodman. (Where have I heard that name before?)

After extensive and varied treatments by Dr. Goodman, Raskal, now past 17, is still enjoying her life very much and no doubt will for some years to come. Dr. Goodman's positive attitude and treatment, Robin's loving care and Raskal's strong will to survive will surely make it so.

Robin made a very good point in her letter to me. Our Senior animals certainly deserve the same concern and respect that our human senior citizens do. In addition, those caring for ailing companion animals need our love and support and prayers every bit as much as if they were caring for a sick human family member. Robin and Raskal, I know there are just loads of good, loving and positive thoughts coming your way from each and every person reading these words!

CRICKET

... this sweetheart enriched the lives of Bea Clements and Annette Woods for 17-1/2 years.

Home Examination

The least stressful way to conduct your frequent examinations of kitty might be to sneak them in during your regular grooming sessions.

Itchy Skin

One of the most common causes for dry, itchy skin can be a deficiency of fatty acids in the diet. But, always check with your vet before making any additions of dietary supplements. As with all our animals, good nutrition means healthy skin and coat.

Mammary Cancer

Hopefully, you are doing all those breast exams regularly, especially if your cat is past age ten. After age ten or twelve, mammary cancer is not at all uncommon. And, it does seem to occur much more frequently in un-spayed cats. Should you feel the presence of any unusual mass in a mammary gland, advise your vet immediately. A little preventative medicine in this department is the early spaying of your cat.

Lyme Disease

This horrendous disease, transmitted by certain species of ticks, puts our outside cats at greater risk — just one more reason for those frequent and regular examinations.

Vaccinations

Our poor, dear kitties have a few of their own dreaded diseases such as Panleukopenia and Feline Leukemia, so those current vaccinations are a MUST. And, their yearly veterinary check-ups will do much to detect early signs of liver and kidney disease, tumors, and dental problems that could become extremely serious. The earlier any of these symptoms are detected, the better are the chances that your kitty will become a happy and healthy Senior.

Urinary Blockage

Male cats are prone to urinary blockage. Most owners mistake the symptom of straining in the litter box for constipation, when it is actually much more serious. The *life threatening situation should be evaluated immediately* by your veterinarian.

Hairballs

Grooming on a *regular* basis will cut down on the amount of hair your cat ingests. Long-haired cats should be brushed *every day*, and even short-haired cats should be brushed *several times a week* to prevent hairballs from forming.

There are commercial products available at pet stores or from your vet that are effective in eliminating hairballs. You just place a dab on the cat's paws and it will be licked off in no time. This is a good preventative measure if your cat has hairballs very often.

Mega-Colon

We had a most informative letter from Carol Pierce. Her 17-year-old cat was experiencing mega-colon with constipation complications. Her veterinarian prescribed Colace, a stool softener; this along with a change in diet and additional water, made life a lot more pleasant for this kitty. Her vet also mentioned that some of her other clients recommended adding cooked pumpkin to a kitty's food; the cats liked it and it was helpful with the constipation problem.

Skin Rash

Carol also wrote about a successful treatment for a kitty's (or dog's) skin rashes caused by flea allergies or heat: Milk of Magnesia® (the original formula, NOT mint) applied directly to the affected area. This had a soothing effect on the burning sensation and should the animal lick off the preparation, it wouldn't prove harmful.

Before trying any of Carol's good suggestions, be sure to check with your own vet for his approval.

EXTRA T.L.C.

COMPASSION AND UNDERSTANDING

PATIENCE + PATIENCE + PATIENCE

WATCHFULNESS

CHAPTER 19

LETTING GO AND EUTHANASIA

Before it is time to let go of an aging and possibly very ill Senior, discuss this topic with your vet. Let him know your wishes, that you never want your pet's life prolonged when she is obviously in pain, distressed, and no longer having any real joy from life. Ask your vet, who probably loves your Senior very much, too, to give you direction when the time is approaching to consider performing euthanasia. You may not realize that you are holding on too long, and your vet's guidance will be invaluable.

Be Present

While you may think you can't possibly be present when your beloved friend is euthanized, please think about it carefully. While it is a traumatic experience of the highest magnitude, it is still so very important that you be with her at the end of your long and wonderful life together. You will be talking to your dear Senior, stroking and calming and reassuring her as she very peacefully and completely painlessly goes to sleep; your loving touch is the last she will feel; your loving voice is the last she will hear.

If you know in your heart that you absolutely cannot handle being present, perhaps it would be best if you could ask a dear friend, one whom your pet has always loved, to be there in your place.

And yes, we all know there is a truly beautiful place known as Pet Heaven!

Home Burial

I have had several of my beloved pets cremated and then have buried the little redwood boxes in various gardens. Sammie lies under a lovely apple tree in San Anselmo, CA; Mandy is below a nice herb garden in the same yard; Sherry is in yet another garden in San Anselmo. While they all remained Californians, with us now in our Oregon garden are some pretty cute and memorable little stone animals which once marked their graves.

Before burying a pet in your yard, it would no doubt be a good idea to check with your local health codes to see that this is allowed.

Organ Transplants

With all the marvelous strides that have been taken in veterinary medicine in the last few years, I believe one day in the not too distant future we will see organ banks for pets, just as they are now a reality for humans. I would gladly consent to the removal and transplant of any organ of a deceased pet, knowing that it could possibly save or prolong the life of someone else's pet.

Autopsy

In the same vein, if an autopsy of my deceased pet could prove beneficial to the veterinary profession, I would gladly give my consent for one to be performed on any of my pets.

If The End Comes At Home

While it will be a devastating and utterly traumatic experience, I do hope that when Pebbles' time comes, I will awaken one morning to find that she has just gone to sleep for the final time. It will certainly be infinitely more easy to handle than if I had to take her to Uncle Doctor for euthanasia.

Should Pebbles become quite ill and it is obvious that her life will soon be over, (*providing* she is in no pain) I would prefer that she be at home for her final hours, rather than in the hospital. I believe that it would be very comforting to my beloved girl to be in the home she loves and with the person she loves the most.

SARA

... a beloved friend from the past, age 16.

This is the saddest of topics but one that must be addressed, especially if there are children in the family. The death of a beloved animal family member need not be a distasteful or frightening experience for children, it could be a way in which to show them that death is not to be feared. I would not doubt that most youngsters would want to be with their beloved friend right up to the end of its life. There would have to be assurance on everyone's part, however, that emotions would be kept in check so that the animal's final hours would be peaceful and quiet.

Extra T.L.C.
Compassion and Understanding
Patience + Patience + Patience
Watchfulness

CHAPTER 20

SOME ENDINGS

Among the many, many letters I received in response to my request for people to share their experiences were a few that told of the end of a beloved pet's life. I shed many tears over many letters, but I believe the one that moved me the most was the story of dear Bijou. I am so grateful to Mimi Scammon for sharing her story with me so that I can share it with you here. Bijou was a silver miniature poodle, who lived to age 17 and had always loved going to the beach and chasing the sea gulls. Bijou's appetite had begun to wane, her eyes had become pretty cloudy and there was stiffness in quite a few joints. This is Bijou's beautiful final day, spent with Mimi:

Bijou

I packed a picnic lunch one beautiful day and Bijou and I went to her beloved beach. We had a lovely day there together, it was real quality time, although she was content just to stroll slowly at my side. The sea gulls no longer amused her (she probably couldn't see them anyway). At sunset, she waded into the surf, up to her chest, then turned to look at me one last time.

She was framed with the glow of a majestic setting sun as she turned toward the sea, took another step or two, then "let go." She actually relaxed, closed her eyes and let the ocean take her. It was what she wanted to do; I realized later she had saved me the agony of the vet visit, the injection, the putting down.

Many people up and down the beach were suddenly at my side, with comforting arms and words of consolation. We stood silently until the sun disappeared.

Would that all our beloved pets could have such a beautiful ending.

Caesar

Another ending that saddened me very much was told to me by a dear, former neighbor in California, Ann Locke. For the twenty-five years that we had been neighbors, I had loved all her kids and I had loved their animals. And Pebbles and Caesar had also known each other a good, long time.

Caesar was a big, handsome, orange cat and the fact that he had lost an eye as a kitten didn't detract a bit from his regal bearing. When Caesar was 14 he quite suddenly lost the sight in the other eye, due to a detached retina. As if that weren't enough to bear, the family learned that Caesar's kidneys were beginning to fail. Being a loving and caring family, they could not have their beloved friend continue his life and endure further pain. Caesar was gently euthanized by Dr. Phil Goebel, with Ann and her girls in attendance. It was a very painful experience, but as Ann said, "We owe it to our pets to be with them at the end of their lives, if it's possible - a small price to pay for their years of love and devotion to us." I agree completely, Ann.

Your Pet's Life After Your Death

How many of us now living with elderly dogs and cats have given serious thought to what will happen to our beloved animals if we should die before they do? It's certainly not a happy thought but one that should be addressed, especially if we are over the age of Social Security. (It should be addressed long before that, in my opinion.) One reads horror stories of people who die, and in their will, they decree that their surviving animals must be put to sleep, too. How sick — what a waste of a dear animal life. Just because a dog or cat has reached Senior status is no reason to believe someone else will not want her and love her for many more years to come.

The best solution, of course, is to make good, solid arrangements for a trusted friend to take the animal, upon your demise, and give it a loving home until the end of it's life. If you are financially able, make suitable arrangements in your will to compensate this friend for the care of your animal. If there is a possession of yours that your friend would love to have, arrange for it to be passed on to the new care-giver of your animal.

If you have, in your wisdom, chosen a dear and trusted friend, remember that person loves your animal almost as much as you always have and will see that it's final years will be full and happy.

Should you not want to put the burden of an animal's care on a friend, there are some wonderful organizations that can be contacted. Most areas have Animal Aid and Animal Rescue organizations. They will be no less diligent in finding a good home for a dog or cat that has reached Senior status, though it may take a bit longer to locate just the right new home. While the search goes on, these animals are lovingly cared for in "foster homes" by the many dedicated volunteers in the organization. Should you choose one of these groups of wonderful people and you are financially able, it might be nice to make a donation to their organization in your will, since almost all of them depend completely on donations to carry on their important work.

Memorial Contributions

When a friend or relative dies, I am completely in favor of memorial contributions to worthy organizations instead of floral remembrances. The flowers will be gone in a day, while the monetary donations will work on and on to benefit the living. In addition to favorite charities that we may have such as the American Cancer Society, Multiple Sclerosis, Cystic Fibrosis, and so many others, I hope you will also remember organizations such as your local Humane Society, Guide Dogs For The Blind, Inc., Hearing Dogs, Canine Companions and Helping Hands, that incredible organization that trains the Rhesus monkeys to assist paraplegics in leading fuller lives. In addition, there are so many wild-life organizations (Wolf Haven is a personal favorite) deserving of all the help we can provide.

Never Say "Never Again"

When your present beloved animal companion has trotted on up to Pet Heaven, PLEASE never ever say, or even think, that you will never have another pet again. Should this thought even remotely cross your mind, I want you to immediately find and read a copy of Eugene O'Neill's classic, *The Last Will And Testament Of An Extremely Distinguished Dog*.

To quote a brief portion of this truly beautiful piece, "It would be a poor tribute to my memory, if after my death, my Mistress decided to never have a pet again. What I need to feel is that, after having had me in her family, she couldn't ever be without another pet."

Please give those profound words a lot of careful thought.

CHAPTER 21

WHEN YOU LOSE YOUR DEAR SENIOR

Only one who has been through the excruciating pain and suffering experienced when a beloved pet dies can understand how completely devastating it can be.

I am a firm believer, and always will be, that the very best way to ease the sorrow we are experiencing is to get a new pet. No new pet will ever take the place of the one we have just lost, and no one could possibly expect it to. But please believe me, a new, devoted, fun, loving dog or cat will do wonders to turn off those tears and help speed the process of ending a deep grief.

Naturally, I recommend adoption with all my heart, either from your local Humane Society or any number of Animal Aid groups. There are truly wonderful dogs and cats of all ages, breeds and all sizes just waiting for YOU to come into their lives.

But, if you really feel that you cannot have a new pet right away, give yourself some time and try some of the following:

- Do some volunteer work at your local Humane Society — they always need extra, loving hands.

- The different Animal Aid and Animal Rescue & Care

groups also are always in need of volunteer help. You might become a foster home to one of their pets awaiting adoption. (You might also, in the process, fall in love with the animal you are temporarily caring for, and voila — everyone ends up a winner!)

- I have read of organizations who help care for AIDS patients' animals, walking their dogs, grooming cats, shopping for pet foods, transporting the animals to vet appointments.

- Depending on where you live, you could be lucky enough to be able to volunteer for such wonderful organizations as Guide Dogs For the Blind, Hearing Dogs, Canine Companion Dogs and similar organizations.

- If you are fortunate enough to live in a community that has a zoo, become a volunteer there — what a treat!

- Visit nursing homes and convalescent homes, preferably with a pet borrowed from a friend. Seek out those patients who have had to give up their beloved pets because of their living situation. You have no idea what joy you will bring into some older lives. When we lived in California, Pebbles and I were members of a wonderful organization called L.I.T.A. [Love Is The Answer]. Each Tuesday we visited one of the convalescent homes, calling on a little friend, Eva Castle-Blanch, God rest her dear soul. It would sometimes take Pebbles and me 10 or 15 minutes to work our way through the lobby and down to Eva's room since just about everyone wanted to touch and speak to this beautiful dog, who no doubt reminded them of dear pets from their past. It was a very moving and gratifying experience for us each week.

- If there is no organization such as the above LITA in your area, perhaps you and some of your friends could be instrumental in starting one! You have absolutely no idea of the joy and love that you could bring into a lot of lives, while enriching your own at the same time.

Just recently I learned of a very important tool to be used while grieving over the death of a beloved pet. It is a videotape on pet loss and your vet may be able to supply it to you. It is produced by the American Animal Hospital Association (AAHA), and they also publish a brochure on the subject. Their address is:

> Grief Brochure, Member Services/AAHA
> P. O. Box 150899
> Denver, COLO 80215-0899
> 303/279-2500

CHAPTER 22

SOME PEOPLE WORTH KNOWING

While some of the people and organizations mentioned can only be enjoyed by us lucky Oregonians, several are located throughout the country.

In the Portland/Beaverton area we are most fortunate to have an organization that is a godsend to pet owners struggling with a variety of problems: behavior, disobedience, aggression, or manners. Mary Lee Nitschke, Ph.D., director of ANIMAL SCHOOL, offers her more than twenty years of experience in animal behavior management and research to her clients. In addition to being able to very successfully improve relationships between people and their pets, ANIMAL SCHOOL also provides a vast range of obedience and training classes for pets of all ages. I've heard some interesting kitty success stories, so this is not a place exclusively for dogs!

Mary Lee Nitschke said something to me I'll always remember:

Think about pets as a way of reducing people stress.

ANIMAL SCHOOL, INC
Koll Business Center, Bldg. 9
7850 SW Nimbus Avenue
Beaverton, OR. 97005
503/646-3060

Most large communities have chapters of PETA (People for Ethical Treatment of Animals). They do so much good work for all animals that it's an organization worth joining.

By the same token, most communities also have SPCA (Society For The Prevention of Cruelty to Animals) chapters. They're always in need of caring volunteers.

Another lady here in the Northwest is Mara Nesbitt of Portland, who has been a state licensed massage therapist for almost 20 years. (In the "Letters" chapter you met her dogs Orion and Zoe.) Mara believes, as I always have, that touching is a very important factor in maintaining a healthy pet. As Mara pointed out, "massaging a pet can help speed recovery from an injury, ease the pain of arthritis in older animals, and, as with humans, provide simple relaxation." She also makes such a logical point when she says, "[In Massage] you're working on the same things whether it's a human or a dog, things such as muscles, tendons, ligaments, the nervous system and the circulatory system." Mara Nesbitt can be reached at 503/292-2214.

Just recently, I heard of a marvelous organization (again just for those of us living in the Portland area, unfortunately). It is called the DOVE LEWIS MEMORIAL EMERGENCY VETERINARY CLINIC. Not only is this a top-rated emergency facility (a non-profit organization founded in 1973), but it also offers a variety of community services that benefit pets and people alike:

Pet Loss Support Group

Lost and Found Pets

Community Education Classes

Pet Visitation Programs

Canine Blood Donor Program

Limited Emergency Care Funding.

It would be worthwhile to call or write for one of their brochures:

Dove Lewis Memorial
Emergency Veterinary Clinic
1984 NW Pettygrove
Portland, OR 97209
503/228-7282

Please don't ever forget your local Humane Society. They almost always need caring volunteers and people to become members. Above all, this is one of the best sources there could be for your next companion animal, be it bird or rabbit, dog or cat, puppy or adult animal.

Just recently, I read one of the best brochures I have ever seen on the subject of older dogs; there is also one published on older cats. I picked up mine in Dr. McCoy's North Portland Animal Clinic, so perhaps they are also available in your own vet's office. The titles are "Care of Old Dogs" and "Care of Old Cats."

EXTRA T.L.C.

COMPASSION AND UNDERSTANDING

PATIENCE + PATIENCE + PATIENCE

WATCHFULNESS

CHAPTER 23

WATCHFULNESS

Remember the little creed that we must all live by when we live with an older or elderly pet?

WATCHFULNESS

EXTRA T.L.C.

COMPASSION AND UNDERSTANDING

PATIENCE + PATIENCE + PATIENCE

WATCHFULNESS

If you were paying careful attention, you will note that I slipped an extra WATCHFULNESS in there. It really is one of the very most important rules in your life right now (especially if you are a dog owner, but cats need lots of it, too).

Out Alone - Unfenced Yard

Never, never let your animal go out the front door without a leash unless the yard is fenced and you are going no further than the yard. An elderly animal won't hear an oncoming car or bike-rider, or the approach of a threatening animal; she also will not see these dangers too well if her eyesight is failing. There could be ditches and other obstructions that could prove harmful to her.

Wandering

The older animal is prone to wander not necessarily out of disobedience but more likely out of forgetfulness of where she had planned on going. And, if her hearing is bad, she won't hear you trying to get her back on track once she has disappeared behind the hedge or the neighbor's garage.

Under-sink Security

Can you remember to what great lengths you went to make your home safe for toddlers: securing doors to under-sink cabinets in kitchens and bathrooms and to storage shelves in laundry rooms. You must take the same precautions for your four-legged kids (young and old) since they are as inquisitive and curious as small children. An old pet with poor eyesight could so easily come upon an open sink cabinet and ingest something that could prove fatal. Some products that can be lethal to animals can have scents that are irresistible to them. And, NEVER let your dog or cat near any garbage material.

Danger Areas

Now is also the time when we must be more aware of other possible danger areas for our Seniors:

- How difficult is it for the animal to negotiate the front and back steps? Would it be wise to be present whenever the pet must use them?

- Is there a ramp area the pet would use and possibly fall off the side? Again, be present during it's use, or modify the ramp.

- Is lawn equipment, such as coiled hoses or potting material, left in areas that could cause a problem with a sight-impaired pet?

- Sliding glass doors — people walk into them all the time. Couldn't a pet do the same? Decals placed on the glass at close to floor level could prevent a painfully bumped nose or forehead.

- When waiting in the waiting-room at your vet's office be certain that no other animal is allowed to approach your's. If the other owners do not have enough common sense to keep their animals on a close leash, go wait in the car or outside the office. This is no time for a nose-to-nose greeting with any animal that could have an infectious ailment.

- Please remember the slippery floors mentioned elsewhere in the book. They can be frustrating and dangerous to an unsteady old Senior.

- An ironing board and the cord of the iron must be used with caution around our elderly animals.

Christmas Time Hazards

While probably everyone knows that poinsettia plants and mistletoe are poisonous to our dogs and cats, there are many others that are as harmful: azalea, boxwood, caladium, Chinaberry tree, daffodil bulbs, diffenbachia, elephant ear, English ivy, holly berries, hyacinth bulbs, hydrangea, oleander, philodendron, and wisteria seeds. Plants that are safe for our animals include spider plant, dracaena, wandering jew and Swedish ivy.

The Christmas holidays are full of hazards for our pets: bobbing ornaments, tree lights and tinsel that can be intriguing to them; ingested gift wrappings and ribbons; turkey bones in garbage that has not been safely disposed of; electrical cords; or frequent door openings afforded by the season's visitors. And remember that a sweet-smelling egg nog holiday drink could be irresistible to an animal. (Thank you, Laird Goodman for these timely tips!)

I have a cousin noted for his outstanding Christmas decorations. The Christmas tree was beautifully and completely decorated and then suspended from the living room ceiling, since there were always several cat members of the family!

Weight Gain Or Loss

A noticeable gain or loss of weight just might be the signal that there is something seriously wrong. Your older animal should be weighed every few months, with weights and dates noted in your trusty little notebook. Any significant changes should be reported to your vet.

EXTRA T.L.C.

COMPASSION AND UNDERSTANDING

PATIENCE + PATIENCE + PATIENCE

WATCHFULNESS

CHAPTER 24

WANNA GO IN THE CAR? (AND OTHER MODES OF TRAVEL)

Difficulty Entering Car

Pebbles entered our car from the rear hatchback until she was no longer able to make that high of a jump. For quite a while it was a simple matter to let her into the car from the rear side door, with the back seat up. I then lowered that half of the seat and she could walk over it and into the hatchback area. Later still, it was sometimes difficult, and no doubt painful, for her to even jump onto the rear seat. I would coax her in until she had her front paws on the seat and then I gently lifted her rear into the car.

If you have a back that flares up once in a while as I do, you might want to try the step-stool approach. I used a small but sturdy wooden box placed on the garage floor by the rear car door. Pebbles could step up on the box, then up to the car seat. This worked fairly well, but she seemed to prefer my lifting her into the car. Before I fashioned the box step-stool, I tried leaning a piece of plywood from the garage floor to the level of the car seat. This was not workable, as she slipped too much on the wood. The idea can be made to work if the plywood is covered either by an old piece of carpet or by stapling an old beach towel to it.

If your large, older animal is still able to jump into and out of the car without your assistance, keep a small throw rug on the garage floor where she will enter and exit to prevent slipping on the slick garage floor. Put some sort of mark on the wall to guide you as you drive into the garage, and when your head is in line with the mark, it's time to stop.

Those of you with the smaller breeds won't face situations such as this and can simply lift the little critter into the car.

Security - Riding In The Car

I've never had a dog yet that didn't love to go in the car with me. Pebbles would rather go in the car and perhaps have to wait for an hour or more than be left home alone. She was always welcome, not only for the good company, but also for the security! No one is going to attempt to hassle a female alone in a car when there is a lot of dog visible a few feet behind her. Even small dogs, who are usually equally protective of an owner, could create such a commotion in a threatening situation that not many "bad guys" would risk the confrontation.

During Pebbles' and my drive from California to Oregon a few years ago, there was an interesting situation involving a group of young men in another car. Pebbles happened to be lying down as I passed their car on the freeway. Shortly thereafter, they began passing me, but then they just kept driving alongside our car. There were a few shouted phrases, a threatening gesture or two; and I was becoming a bit nervous. At that moment Pebbles decided to get up and, being close to fifty pounds, she was pretty visible in the back of the car. The hot-shot cruisers took off rather quickly.

Animal Left In Car

Naturally, everyone knows NEVER to leave an animal in a car on even a warm day, let alone a hot one. The result can very quickly become fatal to a beloved pet. Even with the windows lowered part way, the temperature in an automobile soars *very quickly and very lethally.*

Travel Kit

My car is always equipped with Pebbles' own travel kit. It consists of a water bowl, a capped bottle of fresh water, a spare leash (in case hers is left at home), a jar of emergency kibble, a roll of paper towels (or toilet paper) in a plastic bag, a few plastic bags, and some closing ties. In case of a car breakdown, or a horrendous traffic jam, you will always have the basic necessities for your animal. (I'm sure you know the reason for the paper towels and the plastic baggies.)

Over the past 12 years Pebbles and I have had some wonderful trips together — she is a very good car traveler.

Motels

If you are a AAA member, you can secure a booklet showing the motels/hotels that welcome your pets. Our wonderful freeways have such good rest stops with areas for exercising and pottying your animals. (Be a concerned owner and always clean up after each deposit!) It's a good idea to try to stop every couple of hours when traveling with your animals, and it's good for you, too.

Air Travel

There are times when an animal must travel by airplane. Because it's stressful for an animal at any age I would not use this mode of transportation unless it was absolutely necessary. You must be *assured* by the airline that the baggage area where the pet will travel is pressurized and that it will be neither too hot nor too cold during the flight. Discuss any proposed trip with your vet and he will no doubt supply you with some tranquilizers to be given just before flight time. (Those of you owning small critters can sometimes have the pet with you during the flight.)

Trial Run To The Emergency Clinic

If you are not sure where the nearest emergency veterinary clinic is located, it would be a very good idea to take a trial drive to it long before it might ever be needed. If an emergency exists with an ill or injured animal, you don't want to waste valuable time locating an address with which you aren't familiar.

Blanket As Stretcher

To transport an injured or ill animal to the vet, a blanket works well as a makeshift stretcher when two people are available. (Should the animal be in pain or in shock, it may be necessary to use a muzzle to protect yourself from being accidentally bitten. If no muzzle is available, a long length of wide gauze can be wrapped around the mouth.)

Petravel® Tag

When you're traveling and your animal becomes lost how are you going to make connection if the animal is wearing only your home state identification tag?

Several years ago when traveling north from California with Pebbles, this frightening thought entered my mind and I invented the Petravel® Tag. Should you wish to duplicate my copyrighted idea, it is simple:

Purchase a little plastic luggage marker which attaches to a suitcase with a small metal chain. At the top of the slide-out card, print "I Am Visiting At"; then add the address and phone number of your away-from-home contact. Attach this tag securely to your animal's collar, along with the regular I.D. tag. Leave this extra tag on the collar for the duration of your visit away from home.

When You Must Travel Alone

There are always times when we must travel and our best friends can't be included in the trip. Kenneling is stressful for any animal, but is especially so for an older pet. Do your very best to find a trusted friend to be your animal/house-sitter, rather than using a kennel. The animal is infinitely better off and your plants will get T.L.C., too!

EXTRA T.L.C.

COMPASSION AND UNDERSTANDING

PATIENCE + PATIENCE + PATIENCE

WATCHFULNESS

CHAPTER 25

I AM ONE LUCKY GIRL ... AND I AM 32 YEARS OLD!

Thanks to Dr. Mary Lee Nitschke of the Animal School in Beaverton, I learned of Diana Arnold of Springfield, Oregon and her amazing kitty Lucky Girl who just happens to be 32 years old as of June 1, 1991.

I thought there was going to be one star of this book, but now we will have two stars, Contessa and Lucky Girl.

There are so many amazing things about Lucky that I don't know where to begin. First, she is a mix of Brown Mackerel, Maine Coon and Persian breeds. That in itself sounds pretty impressive to me. Lucky has won over 200 awards, ribbons and trophies in many, many cat shows; she won the Morris Award for Best Household Pet at the annual CFA show in Eugene, Oregon, when she was 27! Lucky has been written up in many magazine and newspapers, among them Cats Magazine (August, 1986) and Globe (September 22, 1987), and she has appeared on Eugene television several times.

Lucky Girl certainly has an appropriate name. If it weren't for her beloved Diana, she would have been put to sleep when she was just 16 years old. Her former owners were moving out of town and had requested that the cat be euthanized. This was far from acceptable to Diana who took Lucky to her vet, Dr. Tim Ramsey of Springfield. He examined the cat, verifying her age and finding a strong and healthy cat that certainly did not need to be put to sleep. Thus began a long and loving relationship between this truly lucky cat and a caring, compassionate woman.

Diana tells me that Lucky's hearing is good, as are her eyesight and her sense of smell. She does have arthritis in her back, hips and legs, but her teeth are still in good condition, although she will no longer eat hard cat food. Because of the arthritis, Lucky finds it difficult to jump "up," so several times a day Diana lifts her up to a favorite window so that she can see what's going on outside. After she has checked out the kids and the birds and squirrels, she can jump "down" unassisted.

Lucky has always been an indoor cat and she rarely gets ill. Usually her only visits to the doctor are for her annual check-ups and her regular booster shots. Her wonderful vet attributes Lucky's longevity to a special diet that Diana worked on for several years to perfect, and to the vitamins she is given. To these two important ingredients, Diana adds peaceful surroundings, tender loving care, and of course, the excellent care of Dr. Ramsey.

Here is Diana Arnold's special diet for Lucky:

> Every fifth day I give her a special gruel containing Brewer's yeast, raw eggs, corn oil, creamed corn, string beans, peas, spinach, canned cat food, water and wheat bread. The rest of the time she eats cat food, cottage cheese, plain yogurt and Swiss cheese.

Dr. Ramsey prescribed a vitamin product that is very important for older cats: Felovite® -II with Taurine. Lucky takes this daily. (Check with your own vet; this may be a product he would suggest for your Senior.)

One of the few signs of old age that Lucky displays is in the litter box, reports Diana: "Ninety percent of the time she doesn't cover her potty. I wind up doing it while she looks on to see what I'm doing. Ten percent of the time she'll make an attempt to cover it. I think she forgets what she's doing at times, and I find her asleep in the potty box. She never makes mistakes — she always uses the potty box."

Lucky is very aware of Diana's health problems. She senses when Diana is not feeling well and will forego her all-morning nap just to be near Diana if needed. This is just one more example of the uncanny ESP that our animals share with us. Once Lucky was curled up in Diana's lap, sound asleep for that regular all-morning nap. She suddenly sat up and began staring at Diana very intently. This went on for several minutes. Diana kept asking Lucky what was the matter, what seemed to be wrong. But Lucky just continued to stare. A very short time later, Diana experienced a medical emergency which lowered her blood pressure dangerously.

Fortunately, everything turned out all right. But, here was just one more incidence of how acutely our animals are tuned in to us.

LUCKY
GIRL

... what an amazing and happy life she has shared with Diana Arnold. As of October, 1991, Lucky is 32 years old!

Diana ended her wonderful letter to me by saying, "Lucky and I have to take one hour at a time. I thank God every day that she lives, that we are together."

I thank Him too, Diana, and I pray that He will give you two some more good years together.

EXTRA T.L.C.
COMPASSION AND UNDERSTANDING
PATIENCE + PATIENCE + PATIENCE
WATCHFULNESS

CHAPTER 26

THOUGHTS IN THE MIDDLE OF THE NIGHT

Pill Time

If your dog or cat is on more than one medication and it is sometimes difficult to keep dosages straight, mark the top of the bottle cap with a felt marker: number of pills, number of times per day, with food or after food, etc.

2 - 2 x day, in F

1 - 3 x day, no F

If it's an ongoing prescription, when you get the new bottle simply remove the old cap and place it on the new bottle.

If an animal's medication is to be given one-half hour before a meal or one hour after, your kitchen timer is a big help.

Storing Pet Food

Purchasing dog or cat kibble in the larger size bags is always more economical. I pour my 35-pound bags into a large, plastic, lidded garbage can which has been lined with a plastic bag. (This is kept in the garage.) I then fill with kibble two large glass containers (with tightly fitting lids) which go back to the kitchen.

With kitties, a smaller plastic garbage can would work well, and could possibly be stored in a pantry.

Freebies

While waiting in various veterinarian's offices, I have picked up so many good, little (free) brochures on all sorts of topics pertaining to our animal's care, including emergency first aid.

Cancer Cause

A very recent article in *The Journal of the National Cancer Institute* contained a study with a frightening conclusion: "Dogs whose owners used a common weed killer on the lawn four or more times a year were twice as likely to develop a deadly type of cancer, Lymphoma." The herbicide is 2,4-D (dichloro-phenoxyacetic acid.) The study didn't mention cats, but this certainly could prove disastrous to our kitties, too. Carefully check labels of any products that you will be using in the garden or on your lawn.

Label Checking

Other labels to be checked carefully are those on our animals' foods. There are an awful lot of unsavory ingredients that go into food that is sold for our dogs and cats; your vet will be happy to give you a list of no-no's to look for in your label-checking.

Jogging Dogs

I almost always feel sad when I see a jogger with a dog in tow. Is that animal really enjoying it as much as the owner hopes she is? Certainly that dog needs the exercise, but not to be able to stop and sniff when she wants to or scratch when she needs to seems like a cruel punishment. I've never yet seen a dog jogging that looked like it was enjoying the episode, but then, come to think of it, the jogger never looks all that happy either. Certainly, an older animal should never be subjected to this strenuous exercise.

Gingko Biloba

If I neglected to mention it previously, GINKGO is the world's oldest living tree species, a deciduous tree which may live as long as 1,000 years. This is the magical ingredient that restored my dog's hearing and I could not have been more grateful at learning of it.

Treats

We all know that special treats for our animals, and in-between-meal snacks are no-no's. However, an acceptable snack is a piece of raw carrot. (Most dogs [I don't know about kitties] love carrots.) I just remembered that my two miniature poodles loved cantaloupe, though they didn't get it too often.

Pill Hiding

Why can't the pill people manufacture brown pills for our dogs and cats? They would be much less noticeable in brown kibble!

Crowded Places

Keep your Senior out of small or crowded places as it is stressful, especially in warm to hot weather.

Hot Weather

Also, in hot weather, if your animal pants continually, she must be kept quiet and cooled down to minimize the danger of heat exhaustion or stroke.

If you must be out of your home for several hours on a hot day and your animal's usual bed area is positioned by a window, lower the blind before you leave so that the bed area is not in bright sun prior to your return. And be certain that her water bowl is always in a sun-free spot.

On a very warm day, you should never walk your animal in the heat of the day; instead, get up early to do it in the cool of the morning, at the same time enjoying some lovely bird sounds. By the same token, on a cold day wait until mid-day when it is warmer for that walk, but don't do it at all if the weather is really cold. Our Seniors don't take kindly to extreme heat or extreme cold. And never forget to tuck several paper towels in your pocket — be a responsible owner.

License Renewal

Where I now live, in Washington County, Oregon, the manner of renewing animal licenses is far superior to what I have always known, a new metal license tag each year. Here, when you send in your renewal fee each year, instead of a new license tag you receive a little paper sticker that is placed on your existing metal tag. Eliminated are the broken finger nails incurred getting the old tag off and the new on, and it is a much more economical way to update the license.

Write To Me!

I would love to hear from you! Write to me in care of my publisher. Perhaps between us we can accumulate enough good information for another book.

Alice Faye

Recently I read about an interview with a great lady, Alice Faye. A memorable comment was "I always say women who live alone should have pets. They're something to make them get up and do things. Too much time on your hands is dangerous."

"Animal"

I would love to see someone start a campaign to get the word animal eliminated from sensational crime stores, i.e. "the criminal acted like an animal." It's ludicrous to use this simile — it's an affront to animals everywhere.

Pebbles' Meals

I don't believe I have ever mentioned what Pebbles eats: 1-1/3 cups Science Diet® Canine Senior (dry kibble) mixed with a scant two tablespoons salt-free chicken broth. Added to this are whatever medications she happens to be on. While she might prefer roast chicken, this is what she is fed for breakfast and dinner, with no snacks in between. Dessert is now two Pet Tabs® Plus (multi-vitamin tablets) which she loves. They are quite large so she gets a couple of good chomps from each one. (Pebbles weighs about 45 pounds.)

I feel that the feeding amounts shown on most bags and cans of pet food are misleading; they usually recommend higher quantities than are advisable. It is best to get the correct amount to feed your animal from Uncle Doctor. (Remember the dirty word — OBESITY.)

Photography For Pets

Also, I don't believe I mentioned that the stunning pictures of Pebbles on the cover of this book, taken by Kathi Lamm, were done when Pebbles was just past 15. The combination of a very photogenic animal and the amazing talents of Kathi really produce some beautiful results. I want you to have Kathi's address in the event that you want to have an outstanding photograph taken of your Senior:

> Kathi Lamm Photography
> P. O. Box 141
> Lake Oswego, Oregon 97034
> 503/650-3820

Eliminate Coat Odor

Do you have a smelly critter from time to time? This is quick, simple and inexpensive, and works for both dogs and cats: baking soda liberally rubbed into the fur. It sort of acts as a dry shampoo in that it will clean and deodorize old stinky at the same time.

Smoking

It's harmful to your dogs and cats. Have you quit yet?

Hearing Loss

The amazing product that I have mentioned for improving an animal's hearing loss, SILICEA 6X, is available in natural food stores. It's priced quite reasonably at around $5.00 for 500 tablets. (Pebbles takes three per day.)

Clothes Dryer Danger

I remember reading a warning about cats and clothes dryers in one of Dr. Mary Lee Nitschke's great columns, "Pets And Their People" which appears in *This Week Magazine*. Since cats love to curl up in warm, soft places, don't let your clothes dryer become a death trap for your beloved pet. If there is a feline in residence at your home, NEVER operate your dryer without first checking to see that there is nothing except laundry in it.

Exercise After Eating

I don't know if it is out-dated or not, but, I have always lived by the rule: never exercise or run an animal right after it has eaten. If you're in doubt, you might want to get your vet's professional opinion.

* * *

If your pet has reached Senior status, congratulations! It probably means that you have given wonderful and loving care to your pets. You have seen that they have eaten only the best foods available, that they have had good veterinary care whenever needed; and you have given your loving time, care and devotion to them all these years.

CHAPTER 27

MENTAL TELEPATHY, OR ESP, OR WHATEVER YOU WANT TO CALL IT, BUT IT'S THERE!

So many of my friends, over the years, have thought "the old girl is off her rocker for sure!" This is their conclusion when I tell them that my animal (Pebbles, more than any other critter I've had) seems to read my mind and know exactly what I am thinking.

So be it ... but the phenomenon has happened too many times and for too many years, for it not to be true. There have been too many instances to mention here (and I don't want you laughing at me, too), but the most frequent and constant ESP between Pebbles and me pertained to our daily walks.

While I was still employed, our daily walks took place when I returned from work. On the week-ends our walks were not so time structured. There were times when I simply had to complete certain chores before I could make the time for Pebbles' walk. I can't begin to list the times when I would be in the bathroom, starting a sauce in the kitchen, reading the morning mail, or talking on the telephone when I would suddenly think, "I just must walk that girl." At the exact moment that that thought entered my mind, Pebbles was at my side, an ebullient look on her face and the big, red tail going a mile a minute! Don't ever try to convince me that our animals don't know what we're thinking and are not tuned into our thoughts!

On numerous occasions on week-ends, while dressing in the morning to go do errands or whatever, I would be deciding to myself if this was a trip Pebbles could go on, too. Just about the time the thought "Sure, she can go, too." entered my mind, Pebbles would appear at the door of the bathroom or bedroom with that "Oh boy, I get to go along!" look on her face. So, have another laugh if you wish, but those are the facts.

EXTRA T.L.C.
COMPASSION AND UNDERSTANDING
PATIENCE + PATIENCE + PATIENCE
WATCHFULNESS

CHAPTER 28

WHY, GRANDMA, WHAT GOOD TEETH YOU HAVE!

We have touched just briefly elsewhere on the importance of good oral hygiene for our dogs and cats, but since having met Donald McCoy, DVM of the North Portland Animal Clinic recently, I now have an abundance of excellent advice on the subject for you.

Dr. McCoy, renowned in the field of Veterinary Dentistry in the Portland area, has done several papers on the subject and has graciously given me permission to quote from some of them for your benefit.

> Oral hygiene is just as important for our pets as it is for any other member of our family, and more and more health problems are thought to be complicated by an animal's bad teeth. In fact, dental care is one of the most important preventative measures we can do for our pet's health.
>
> Plaque and tartar build up on a pet's teeth just as on our own teeth. (Dogs tend to be more susceptible to the buildup than cats.) Bacteria develop in the

plaque and begin to do damage, especially in the crevices between the teeth and gums. This can lead to gum infections called gingivitis and can progress to periodontal disease. Besides the obvious problems of tooth abscesses and cavities, infections from infected teeth and gums can be absorbed by the blood stream and can be the cause of numerous health problems, including heart and kidney disease.

We certainly don't need to give our more vulnerable Seniors one more hurdle to face.

Here are some signs of periodontal disease:

- a persistent, foul, mouth odor
- red gums that may be swollen or tender to touch
- pus between the gums and teeth (pyorrhea)
- loose teeth

If any of the above signs are present in your pet's mouth, a visit to your veterinarian is in order immediately.

Since 1982, veterinary dentistry has become a specialty all its own; and amazingly, but thankfully, veterinarians are now doing root canals, using braces and bite plates to move teeth, and generally making a lot of critters' mouths healthier and happier.

If you've ever experienced the sheer, unadulterated joy of a root canal, I believe that you would do just about anything under the sun to see that no Senior of yours ever faces the prospect of one. Consequently, the happy alternative of good preventative dental care is suddenly most attractive! For years, every vet I have ever known has advocated brushing the teeth of my animals. According to Dr. McCoy, "brushing them even once or twice per week can be extremely beneficial to a healthy mouth, thereby insuring a more pleasant 'kiss' hello from our animals." There is a safe and pleasant way to go about brushing the teeth, and your vet will be more than happy to instruct you, including advising the proper cleaning agents to use. (After you become proficient in the brushing department, please let me know if you were able to teach your critter to rinse and spit.)

One further bit of information, courtesy of Dr. McCoy, concerns bones for our animals:

> Though I generally do not recommend bones for your pet, I make the exception concerning *knuckle bones*. As a preventative dental measure, ten to fifteen minutes per WEEK of gnawing on these large, hard bones will help clean tartar and keep gums healthy. Because the bones are so hard, do not allow the dog to chew longer than 15 minutes, as the teeth can fracture. Dry food, rawhide and milkbone treats will not prevent dental disease appreciably. However, canned food will hasten the process in both dogs and cats.

Please make note and adhere to Dr. McCoy's very definite lengths of time and frequency of allowed chewing.

The reason for my meeting with Dr. McCoy was the necessity of some dental care for Pebbles. As she had to be anesthetized for the procedure, I had a rather drunk dog who was pretty unsteady on her feet for several hours. In order to assist her in going "out," I looped a big bath towel under her belly and, holding on to the ends, walked her out to the yard. It helped quite a bit as it seemed to give her some confidence.

CHAPTER 29

PARTY TIME

Our old and elderly pets need as little stress in their lives as possible.

My dogs have always been very people-orientated and loved parties with lots of people. As they grew older and as I learned the importance of eliminating as much stress in their lives as possible, I changed my tactics in entertaining.

To eliminate the stress of having to respond to each ring of the doorbell, I confined the pet to a bedroom as far away from the front door as possible. (You might even consider disconnecting the doorbell on party day or night.)

The pet's bed was placed in this bedroom, along with fresh water and a couple of favorite toys. I would go in from time to time to reassure her that I was still there and that she would be coming out soon. (If there are children among the guests one of them, of whom the animal is particularly fond, might just love to play baby-sitter.)

And, on the subject of parties, you might have to strongly insist to your guests that under no *circumstances* is your animal to be slipped any party goodies. Explain firmly, but good-naturedly, that your animal's diet is strictly regulated and there is no place for chips and dips in her menu.

Once, at a Christmas party, I observed a so-called good

friend offering Pebbles some smoked salmon pate on a cracker. When I blew up, he explained that all dogs love fish and he just couldn't resist those begging eyes. Perhaps the salmon wouldn't be too harmful, but she most certainly did not need the accompanying cream cheese, mayonnaise and cracker.

I thought I had made my point, but a short time later there was a sneaky repeat performance. The "good friend" was asked, in no uncertain terms, to leave the party. In my estimation, the loss of this friendship was hardly as important to me as was my dog's continuing good health and well-being.

The story has a happy ending. The following day a lovely floral arrangement was delivered to Pebbles and me, along with a most apologetic note.

If your pet is going to be around the guests and not separated from the festivities, feed her a lighter dinner than usual. Then make available a *small* supply of the pet's regular kibble, to be doled out sparingly by those guests who simply cannot resist your dog's begging eyes. But the best solution, by far, is no snacks at any time — just regular meals and at regular meal times.

As for liquor … anyone who would offer liquor in any form to an animal is an imbecile. Should one of these clods inadvertently slip into one of your parties, make no excuses; make no apologies; simply kick the jerk out the nearest exit.

(Should flowers arrive the next day, refuse delivery!)

CHAPTER 30

SLEEPING LATE

If you're a working person, what do you do in the mornings when you must get up early and go to work and your pet doesn't want to arise for another two hours?

- Let sleeping beauty stay in bed until about 20 minutes before you must leave; then awaken her, let her out, feed her breakfast and let her out again, if needed.

- Have a trusted friend or neighbor come over on work mornings to do the necessary chores.

- I would never recommend fixing the breakfast, the fresh water and the dog/cat door if you use one and then leaving for work. It would be too stressful for an animal to wake up and find you gone.

EXTRA T.L.C.
COMPASSION AND UNDERSTANDING
PATIENCE + PATIENCE + PATIENCE
WATCHFULNESS

CHAPTER 31

THE BIG, GOOD WOLF

For years I have loved wolves; I've been so impressed with their devoted family structure, their magnificent beauty, their ability to survive under the awesome conditions and obstacles that man has placed before them for so many years.

My family room, "The Critters Room," boasts walls covered with stunning color photographs and a couple of prized prints of wolves by outstanding wildlife artists. I have some thrilling videos of wolves, as I videotape everything that ever appears on television pertaining to them. My videos *Dances With Wolves* and *White Fang* may have to be replaced one of these days, I have run them so often.

When I moved to Oregon in 1989, I learned that people breed and sell hybrid wolves as family pets, and I was amazed at the number of classified ads there were offering their sale. As Pebbles was getting on in years, I began to give some thought to whom my next best friend would be once she had trotted on up to Pet Heaven. How thrilling it would be to have a part-wolf animal as my next companion!

After giving a lot of thought to the exciting possibility of owning a wolf-dog, my better judgment took over as I started to consider how others might feel if I gave in to this burning desire. I have several lovely neighbors with small children and I worried that my having a partly wild animal in my home could cause them quite a bit of concern. In addition, I discussed my desire with one of my veterinarians, also a real wolf lover, and was given very sound advice: "Don't do it."

This vet knew of several wolf-dogs who turned out to be wonderful family pets, but there were also many who did not. It would be just too great a chance to take. I valued the extensive and logical advice I was given and decided that my intense desire to be close to a wolf could be fulfilled in other ways.

My desire *was* fulfilled just recently when I visited WOLF HAVEN! I had heard of this wonderful spot for several years from my dear sister, Bonnie in California, but it wasn't until I became an Oregonian that I was close enough to pay it a visit. (Wolf Haven is only about a two hour drive from Portland.) My first visit (one of what will be many, I know) was one of the most unforgettable experiences of my life. During the guided tour of the many huge wooded enclosures where the wolves live, one is lucky enough to be within four or five feet of these beauties; so picture taking is super. The knowledgeable tour guide gives one such marvelous insight into the lives of the animals: how they happened to arrive at Wolf Haven, the history of their species. Then she turns you green with envy as she scratches Lucan behind the ears or rubs the belly of Clementine! There is such devotion displayed between the wolves and the volunteer guides.

Wolf Haven has a beautiful brochure, filled with excellent information and some stunning pictures of the animals. I would like to quote from it here:

> Wolves have had an unfair rap. From such childhood stories as Little Red Riding Hood, millions of us have been led to perceive the wolf as a villainous creature. Movies and television have had a field day perpetuating the wolf as the four-legged bad guy.
>
> The truth is something else: Wolves are social animals living together in a tightly knit group. While only

one female has pups, the rest of the pack pitches in when it comes to providing for their care. Contrary to their savage image, wolves show much affection for each other. In the wild they are afraid of humans, sometimes not even crossing the path where one has walked.

Wolves were once found in all parts of the United States, and Canada. As top predators in a complex web of life, they played a role in maintaining nature's diversity. They helped perpetuate healthy populations of deer, elk and other species. They contributed to keeping other smaller predators from becoming over abundant, which in turn prevented other species from being excessively preyed upon. While they did not attack man, occasionally they did take unattended domestic stock.

Through excessive hunting, poisoning and trapping, the wolf was eliminated from much of its range. Gone are the Japanese, Newfoundland, Central European and Kanai wolves. Lingering on are the Indian, Italian, Scandinavian and Mexican wolves. In the lower forty-eight states the wolf has been reduced to less than 0.1% of its original population and eradicated from almost all of the National Parks.

Today the wolf is starting to make a comeback, and you can help. Wolf Haven's mission is wolf conservation through education, research and outright caring. On a direct level it has taken in more than 40 captive wolves in desperate need of homes, and provided them wooded enclosures on a spacious 65 acre sanctuary.

The wolves at Wolf Haven serve as ambassadors for their kind. Annually over 25,000 people take part in guided sanctuary tours, learning about the wolf's fascinating social behavior and struggle to survive in the wild.

Wolf Haven reaches out to innumerable school, civic and professional groups. Its membership is more than 10,000 strong. It produces an exciting, informative quarterly newsletter. The media, too, has been very helpful to our cause, reaching out to millions.

Research which aids wolf conservation is strongly encouraged. Wolf Haven has pulled together a panel of experts representing a broad spectrum of government and non-government wildlife agencies, as well as professionals from environmental associations, universities and related institutions. Wolf Haven supported scientific investigations in northern British Columbia, Canada, where wolf control is a major issue. It helped in the fight against the same day shooting of wolves sighted from airplanes in Alaska, which brought about changes in policy.

As an aid in documenting wolf recovery, Wolf Haven has trained field biologists from several states to recognize signs of wolf and coyote. One of the most exciting programs has been the development of a volunteer wolf howling brigade which spends its summer weekends systematically carrying out howling surveys over hundreds of square miles in the Cascade mountains where further proof of wolf presence is needed.

How Can You Help?

You can be a part of the important work of Wolf Haven and share in our enjoyment of the wolf by adopting one of our wolves. When you do, you will help pay for it's food, medical care, and the upkeep of the grounds and enclosures.

GET INVOLVED

ADOPT A WOLF

JOIN AS A MEMBER

PARTICIPATE AS A VOLUNTEER

TOGETHER WE *CAN* MAKE A DIFFERENCE

I hope you will want to write to Wolf Haven for one of these lovely brochures which will include a membership form for your use. Their address is:

WOLF HAVEN
3111 Offut Lake Road
Tenino, Washington 98589

For more information call 1-800-GIV-WOLF (448-9653) or save Wolf Haven the cost of the call by telephoning 206/264-4695.

When you receive your brochure, be sure to look for Windsong, an unbelievably beautiful Buffalo Wolf — she's mine! (But I will share her with other adoptive Moms.)

If your local zoo is fortunate enough to have wolf inhabitants, they very often also have adopt-an-animal plans, another way in which you can become involved with these important members of our land.

* * *

We should all be aware that wolves DO NOT make good pets. They are wild animals. Hybrid wolf-dogs also DO NOT make good pets. They are not wild animals, but they are not really tame, either. Unlike wolves, hybrids do not have a fear of humans, and they may see us as any other animal — potential prey. As with any prey, they attack the weak and the young. This accounts for the tragic stories that we have all read of attacks on small children who approach the hybrids. Hybrids, if released into the wild, will deplete the gene pool of true wolves by breeding with them. In this way, wolf populations in the wild are reduced.

* * *

Just once — before I die — I pray that I will have the opportunity to approach a wolf, be accepted by it, and give it a gentle, loving hug.

WINDSONG

... this is my beautiful adopted wolf who lives at Wolf Haven, Tenino, Washington. And I will share her with other adoptive moms!

Extra T.L.C.
Compassion and Understanding
Patience + Patience + Patience
Watchfulness

TO ORDER:

If your local bookstore is out of *Yes, Virginia ... There is a Pet Heaven*, you may order directly from Pebbles Publishing by sending your check in the amount of $12.95 + $2.00* for postage and handling to:

> Pebbles Publishing
> P.O. Box 1432
> Beaverton, OR 97075-1432

Thank you and happy, happy reading!

EXTRA **T.L.C.**
COMPASSION AND UNDERSTANDING
PATIENCE + PATIENCE + PATIENCE
WATCHFULNESS

*For each additional book ordered, please add $.50 postage.